Trust within reason

Some philosophers hold that trust grows fragile when people become too rational. They advocate a retreat from reason and a return to local, traditional values. Others hold that truly rational people are both trusting and trustworthy. Everything hinges on what we mean by 'reason' and 'rational'. If these are understood in an egocentric, instrumental fashion, then they are indeed incompatible with trust. With the help of game theory, Martin Hollis argues against that narrow definition and in favour of a richer, deeper notion of reason founded on reciprocity and the pursuit of the common good. Within that framework he reconstructs the Enlightenment idea of citizens of the world, rationally encountering, and at the same time finding their identity in, their multiple commitments to communities both local and universal.

D1516389

Trust
within reason

MARTIN HOLLIS

Professor of Philosophy in the School of Economic and Social Studies,
University of East Anglia

CAMBRIDGE
UNIVERSITY PRESS

PUBLISHED BY THE PRESS SYNDICATE OF THE UNIVERSITY OF CAMBRIDGE
The Pitt Building, Trumpington Street, Cambridge CB2 IRP, United Kingdom

CAMBRIDGE UNIVERSITY PRESS
The Edinburgh Building, Cambridge CB2 2RU, United Kingdom
40 West 20th Street, New York, NY 10011–4211, USA
10 Stamford Road, Oakleigh, Melbourne 3166, Australia

Based on the inaugural series of A. C. Reid Lectures
in Philosophy at Wake Forest University

First published 1998

Printed in the United Kingdom at the University Press, Cambridge

Typeset in Monotype Dante 10.5 / 13.75 pt, in QuarkXPress™ [SE]

A catalogue record for this book is available from the British Library

Library of Congress Cataloguing in Publication Data
Hollis, Martin.
    Trust within reason / Martin Hollis.
        p.   cm.
    Includes index.
    ISBN 0 521 58346 2 (hardback)
    ISBN 0 521 58681 x (paperback)
    1. Trust (Psychology) – Social aspects.   2. Confidence – Social
aspects.   3. Reason.   I. Title.
BJ 1533.C6H65   1998
179'.9 – DC 21

CONTENTS

Trust within reason is based on the inaugural series of A. C. Reid
Lectures in Philosophy at Wake Forest University and I take pleasure in
giving thanks to all who made the occasion possible. For almost half a
century Dr Reid so inspired his students at Wake Forest that it was
decided to mark his death with a fitting memorial. The A. C. Reid
Philosophy Endowment Fund, whose subscribers include many of
those students, exists to promote a philosophical spirit in a troubled
world and the A. C. Reid Lectures are part of its endeavours. I am glad
to be associated with so noble an undertaking and honoured to have
been invited to inaugurate the series. It was a very genial occasion too,
widely attended and leading to fertile exchanges with members of
several departments. That is due to the Wake Forest Philosophy
Department and I thank the philosophers for the energy and kindness
which went into the accompanying arrangements. Ralph Kennedy
and Win-Chiat Lee, in particular, who undertook the practical work,
were tireless in their determination to make the lectures a success and
their visitor abundantly welcome.

The final text also owes much to a period in Munich as the guest of
the Philosophy Department and especially to the comments of my

amiable host, Wilhelm Vossenkuhl. That provided a welcome chance to extend and improve the text, helped by wide-ranging seminars with graduates and faculty. Raimo and Maj Tuomela, who were visiting the University, kindly shared their work on joint action and gave me the benefit of their comments.

I am also grateful, as always, to my colleagues at the University of East Anglia, particularly to Timothy O'Hagan, who has been an invaluable critic for very many years and improved the text on this occasion too, to Roberta Sassatelli, who was acute in her comments, and to Robert Sugden, my sterling compass through the thickets of the theory of games. Jerry Goodenough has kindly prepared the bibliography and index.

Finally, very special thanks are due to Rüdiger Bittner, who was researching at East Anglia while I was writing the original lectures and, with unstinted generosity, has subjected more than one draft to a precise and stimulating scrutiny. I have gained hugely from his unflagging queries and suggestions, to say nothing of the pleasures of philosophy in his company. The final text does not rise to the standards which he sets but has improved vastly in the attempt.

1

The paradox of trust

John Locke declared trust to be 'the bond of society', the *vinculum societatis*, and we need not doubt him.[1] Everyday life is a catalogue of success in the exercise of trust. Our dealings with friends and enemies, neighbours and strangers depend on it, whether in homes, streets, markets, seats of government or other arenas of civil society. Would you ask a stranger the time unless you could normally count on a true answer? Could you use the highway without trusting other drivers? Could an economy progress beyond barter, or a society beyond mud huts, unless people relied on one another to keep their promises? Without trust, social life would be impossible and there would be no philosophers to try casting the light of reason upon it.

But, although trust is an obvious fact of life, it is an exasperating one. Like the flight of the bumblebee or a cure for hiccoughs, it works in practice but not in theory. When we think about it, the obvious fact that, on the whole, we manage to live together in mutual confidence

1. *Essays on the Laws of Nature* (1663), ed. W. von Leyden, Oxford: Clarendon Press, 1954, p. 213. Locke argues that self-interest cannot be the basis of 'the law of nature' and I warmly applaud. I would like to thank John Dunn for the reference.

turns mysterious. In *Essays on the Law of Nature*, Locke accounted for trust by invoking a divinely ordained 'rule of morals or law of nature', which makes us trustworthy when we are acting in conformity with it. This ordinance, discernible through sense experience by the light of nature and binding on us, lets us see what does and does not accord with our rational nature. In the more famous *Essay Concerning Human Understanding* he made it a matter of appeal to nature without recourse to God's will.[2] But, either way, reference to an external moral fabric for our lives no longer satisfies philosophers outside the natural law tradition. Modern philosophy of a kind which counts Locke among its founders largely subscribes to an Enlightenment view of reason and nature, of knowledge and reality, requiring a more profane account of trust. Even so, the light of reason should have no trouble in illuminating the bond of society. But it does.

The trouble may be with the light, especially if we construe practical reason as instrumental or 'economic' rationality. It may be that it is not instrumentally rational to trust instrumentally rational people. If so, we need a better account of reason, as I shall urge presently, and one which does not spread distrust as more people come to accept it. On the other hand, it may be because the bond of society defies reason in any version. This thought is especially disturbing, given current fears that the bonds of liberal society are growing more fragile. I do not just mean fears that crimes of violence are on the increase and neighbourhoods becoming less safe after dark. I mean also more abstract fears that social changes are eroding people's sense of trust and of belonging, thus making them blind to the needs of others and less willing to contribute to the common weal.

If such anxieties are well grounded, there are two diagnoses. One is that trust grows fragile when people become too rational; the other that trust grows fragile when people are not rational enough. Both are plausible and the difference between them cuts very deep. They imply different accounts of practical reason, together with different ideas of

---

2. 1690, or the Oxford: Clarendon Press edition, ed. P. H. Nidditch, 1975.

law, politics, social science and the conduct of personal life. One bids us be more rational, the other less.

For a view that reason undermines trust, here is Francis Fukuyama, author of *Trust: The Social Virtues and the Creation of Prosperity*.[3] This popular book contrasts societies where there is a 'cultural community' with those which lack 'cultural capital'. The former secure trust through a solidarity which depends not on explicit rules and regulations but on 'a set of ethical habits and reciprocal moral obligations internalised by each of the community's members'. The latter are typically those where economic rationality has made such inroads into social cohesion that, perversely, they cannot exploit the economic opportunities created by their rationality. Hence there is a political message too:

> if the institutions of democracy and capitalism are to work, they must coexist
> with certain pre-modern cultural habits that ensure their proper functioning.
> Law, contract and economic rationality provide a necessary but not a sufficient
> basis for the prosperity of post-industrial societies; they must be leavened with
> reciprocity, moral obligation, duty toward community and trust, which are
> based in habit rather than rational calculation.

Fukuyama thus contrasts reason and modern legalism with habit and pre-modern social virtues. Whereas efficiency depends on the former, trust depends on the latter. We need both, he says, and prosperity depends on striking a balance.

His way of construing the bond of society bodes ill, however. If reason is modern and if trust depends on a habit of practising some pre-modern social virtues, then it is no surprise to find trust becoming fragile. Rationality thus conceived can hardly fail to subvert ancient trust – pre-modern reciprocity, moral obligation, duty to community – which is based in habit. If reason is the voice of progress, it threatens to ruin us all.

This is no way to keep our philosophical spirits up at the end of a

---

3. *Trust: The Social Virtues and the Creation of Prosperity*, New York: The Free Press, 1995. Quotations below are from chapter 2.

troubled century. But, before stating the contrary view, I shall mark out the scope and strategy of *Trust Within Reason*. Trust is a huge topic, ramifying throughout the social sciences and humanities. The core problem is how it can and should be achieved, given what Kant termed 'man's asocial sociality', and I shall address it. But, since a philosopher would be rash to claim expertise across the board, my title signals a particular slant. *Trust Within Reason* asks what reason can tell us about the basis of trust. By 'reason', I mean both a broad Enlightenment idea that we have powers of theoretical and practical reasoning which can guide us in what we believe and do, and a precise current version of it, whose better name is perhaps 'rationality'. This is the instrumental notion at the heart of rational choice theory, game theory and an 'economic' approach to human behaviour. Connecting the general to the particular is a persistent question of whether the spread of reason (or rationality) enlightens the modern world or undermines the trust between people which makes it possible.

Here is my theme, stated broadly. We cannot flourish without trust. This should be as plain to reason as it is to common sense. So reason should be able to show us what makes for a reliable social order, where people find it rational to trust one another. Yet, at least in some current versions, it apparently bids us play the games of social life in ways which make losers of us all. This applies especially to the suggestion that trust is a matter of mutual self-interest. However plausible it sounds, it subverts the bond of society by challenging the utility of social virtues like public spirit, neighbourliness, honour, common decency and, in a word, reciprocity. Is that because these are moral notions, potent only when protected by custom and habits and thus shielded from the light of reason? There are those who say so. But they are not straightforwardly moral notions in a sense approved by most moral philosophers. They are neither abstract enough to be clearly universal nor uncontentious enough in their claim to be virtues. Honour, for instance, is a powerful but local social adhesive which often licenses morally questionable conduct. Yet trust can seem to depend on local ties which it is neither instrumentally rational nor morally commendable to respect. In that case, there cannot be trust within reason. But, given a different idea of practical reason, deeper than prudence and morally charged, we shall find that the light of reason illuminates the bond of society after all.

The slant is thus that reason, when wrongly defined, can distort what it is meant to illuminate. A theory of practical reason tells us how we do and should reach conclusions about what to do. An instrumental theory makes prudence the guide and tells us when it is rational to trust people guided by prudence. That means, roughly, that we can trust people to do what best furthers their aims and to avoid what does not. There is a sting in the tail, since this makes it rational to act in a trustworthy way less often than it takes to sustain a general trust. So the more people adopt the theory, the more fragile the bond of society becomes. Hence, as a descriptive theory, its truth depends on how widely it is believed; and, since believing it has implications for what it is rational to do, it is, so to speak, a player in the game which it analyses. That makes it also a normative theory but not yet a true one. When we ask what would be true, part of the answer comes with seeing how people act in the light of different theories. So can we find a theory of practical reason which leads us to trust one another when we know that we share it? If so, that will be a happy ending.

By keeping trust within reason, a philosopher may, I hope, venture within range of prowling social theorists far more expert in understanding human relationships. But I do not thereby endorse a division of labour between philosophers and others, which assigns an exclusive expertise to each. A sub-theme will be that boundaries between philosophy, social theory and social science are inherently fluid, perhaps merely artificial, because we are part of our own subject matter and belong to a world which changes as intellectual boundaries become known to change. In asking what a world would be like where there is trust within reason, we help or hinder its construction.

TRUTH, VIRTUE AND HAPPINESS

With this preamble, I turn to the other side of the question about the roots of trust, the view that trust is fragile because we are not rational enough. When the *philosophes* of the eighteenth century were assembling what has come to be called the Enlightenment project, they were sure that there is truth to discern about the nature of our social ties, bonds and, to add a key term, obligations. It was, they presumed, a scientific truth, even if the social sciences were too young to discern it in full. Where trust flourishes, people must have reasons to trust one another and one task for the young moral sciences was to identify the character and workings of such reasons. Where trust is fragile and the bond of society weak, a rational understanding of the bond can tell us how to strengthen it. As the moral sciences progressed, it would become clear how social obligations function, thus explaining how societies work and revealing how they can work better. Whereas today's readers may jib at this joining of 'is' and 'ought', the Enlightenment project for human progress took a future moral science to be seamless. A science of morals which studied the essential character of human nature and the forms which morality takes in practice would identify the true virtues whose cultivation increases human wellbeing. The presumption was, in short, that 'truth, virtue and happiness are bound together by an unbreakable chain'.

Enlightenment scholars will recognise this note of vaulting optimism about reason and progress. The proposition that 'truth, virtue and happiness are bound together by an unbreakable chain' comes from a remarkable book, the *Sketch for a Historical Picture of the Progress of the Human Mind*.[4] The *Sketch* is often acclaimed as the purest, boldest and noblest statement of the Enlightenment project. Its author, the Marquis de Condorcet (1743–94), was a philosopher, mathematician, social scientist and supporter of the French Revolution of 1789. Although belonging to an aristocracy unenthused by a revolution which guillotined aristocrats, Condorcet saw in it the dawning of an enlightened age. Proscribed under the Terror in 1793, he went into hiding, where he wrote the *Sketch* in great haste as an outline for what would have been a massive work. In 1794 he was discovered and

4. Marie-Jean-Antoine-Nicolas Caritat, Marquis de Condorcet, *Sketch for a Historical Picture of the Human Mind* (1795), ed. Stuart Hampshire, trans. June Barraclough, Westport, Conn.: Greenwood Press, 1955.

arrested by the *gendarmes* of the revolution he proclaimed, and he died in prison two days later. The book was published in 1795 by his Jacobin friends as an enduring testament to his and their faith in reason and a better world.

The *Sketch* divides human history into ten stages, of which the ninth runs from Descartes to the French Revolution and the tenth is described in the future tense. Condorcet links truth, virtue and happiness from the start. 'Man is born with the ability to receive sensations', he begins, promptly adding that from this capacity and an ability to form and combine ideas 'there arise between him and his fellow creatures ties of interest and of duty, to which nature herself has wished to attach the most precious portion of our happiness and the most painful of our ills'. This is the cue for new moral and political sciences, which will have direct implications for morals and politics, and he undertakes to demonstrate 'how nature has joined together indissolubly the progress of knowledge and that of liberty, virtue and respect for the natural rights of man' (p. 10).

The theme is resumed at the start of the ninth stage, where he assures us that 'publicists have at last discovered the true rights of man and how they can all be deduced from the single truth that *man is a sentient being, capable of reasoning and of acquiring moral ideas*' (p. 128). The true rights are those needed to secure the interests of each and all. Our interests are simple: happiness in the first instance and, to achieve it, prosperity, liberty and greater equality of wealth, education and opportunity. There is no reason in nature or human nature why they should conflict. Where they seem to, it is a sign that our feelings are misdirected and our institutions imperfect. The new sciences will teach us to school the former and improve the latter. Taking stock of human progress, as he reaches his own century, he assures us that 'All errors in politics and morals are based on philosophical errors and these in turn are connected with scientific errors' (p. 163). Then, looking ahead to a sunlit, if distant, future, the final chapter promises that 'The time will therefore come when the sun will shine only on free men who know no other master than their reason' (p. 179).

The method proposed is thus to assume that all human beings have the same universal human nature and capacities, to understand how we form ideas and then to guide us to progressive ones. This is one prong of a scientific campaign to improve our perfectible nature, as indicated by this rhetorical question:

> Just as the mathematical and physical sciences tend to improve the arts that we use to satisfy our simplest needs, is it not also part of the necessary order of nature that the moral and political sciences should exercise a similar influence upon the motives that direct our feelings and our actions? (p. 192)

The other is to shape public institutions and laws to create a public realm which works for human benefit, portended by further rhetorical questions:

> What are we to expect from the perfection of laws and public institutions consequent upon the progress of those sciences but the reconciliation, the identification of the interests of each with the interests of all? Has the social art any other aim save that of destroying their apparent opposition? Will not a country's constitution and laws accord best with the rights of reason and nature when the path of virtue is no longer arduous and when the temptations which lead men from it are few and feeble? (p. 192)

With this triumph of reason in prospect, the book ends with a moving peroration:

> How consoling for the philosopher who laments the errors, the crimes and the injustices which still pollute the earth and of which he is often the victim is this view of the human race, emancipated from its shackles, released from the empire of fate and from that of enemies of its progress, advancing with a firm and sure step along the path of truth, virtue and happiness. (p. 201)

Two centuries later, injustices still pollute the earth and we have yet to acknowledge enlightened reason as our only master. We may wonder why the path is proving so hard. Condorcet would no doubt diagnose 'enemies of progress' on the one hand and scientific ignorance or error on the other. But there are other answers, far less consoling for the philosopher. One is that errors in morals and politics do not all rest on philosophical errors and so on scientific errors in the way envisaged by Condorcet, and this thought will engage us later.

Meanwhile, here is a more frightening answer. It is that the Enlightenment project, so blithely sketched in the Age of Reason, rests on a catastrophic mistake. For, far from being the friend of virtue and happiness, reason is their enemy. If the French Revolution is hailed as a new dawn of reason applied to human nature and society, then notice that the dawn began with a bloodbath, dictatorships and wars throughout Europe, before achieving a far from perpetual peace. Since then, the new social sciences have certainly increased the power and scope of reason; but notice how they have somehow conferred it on tyrants like Hitler and Stalin, whose state machinery has used truth to destroy virtue and happiness. It is not the sleep of reason which begets monsters, as in Goya's famous painting, but reason itself.

This chilling retort is too stark for the theme which I wish to explore but I include it as a backdrop to the ambivalence about reason which so many thinkers have felt. Enlightenment banishes whatever it regards as superstition, prejudice, corruption and the misuse of power and it promises a rationally ordered society of rational individuals. But, in giving its disciples the power to bring rational order about, it takes a great risk. The risk is partly that, by conceding nothing to a human nature which is stubbornly imperfect, it dismantles old defences against original sin, and so lets the devils expelled from the front door take control when they return by the back. The grimmer risk is that reason is itself the enemy of human qualities and relations which a just, free and good society must cherish, the enemy of trust.

In that case – and this is my theme – we should be wary of a society where free individuals know no other master than their reason, if 'reason' is construed in some typically modern ways. We should also be wary of social sciences, built on a particular model of the natural sciences, which are then licensed to shape our motives and institutions in the hope of identifying the interests of each with the interests of all. Hence we may wonder whether we have been misled in philosophy too, and thus come to embrace post-modern doubts about the universal and objective character of reason, especially in its pretensions to moral progress. Yet such doubts are not conclusive. Even if some ways of construing the notion of rationality in Enlightenment spirit make it irrational to trust people who are rational, there may be other notions on offer. Truth, virtue and happiness may still be ours to connect in some manner. Let us see.

THE PROBLEM OF TRUST

With these large thoughts in the background, I shall next focus on what the title of the chapter terms 'the paradox of trust'. To locate it, let us resume the more ordinary thought that trust is essential for everyday life and pervades our dealings with friends and enemies, neighbours and strangers. Whenever we eat, drink or close our eyes, we trust others not to harm us. Every day is an adventure in trusting thousands of others, seen and unseen, to act reliably. Would you exchange your old car for my pile of bank notes if you thought I might have printed the notes in my cellar? Well, you might risk it if you knew your old car was all rust under the new paint. Fraud is a fact of life too. But fraud depends upon honesty in general and, taking our bearings from what constitutes the bond of society, we readily grant the overall need for bank notes to be genuine and second-hand cars what they seem.

We can provisionally distinguish two varieties of trust. (Whether they are finally distinct will be discussed later.) Firstly, we trust one another to behave predictably in a sense which applies equally to the natural world at large. I trust my apple tree to bear apples, not oranges. I trust its boughs to bear my weight, if they look strong and healthy. I trust my reliable old alarm clock to wake me tomorrow, as it did yesterday. I trust you to wear a blue shirt again today, never having seen you in anything else. These are inductive inferences, reliable but, as every philosopher knows, not guaranteed, and trust is a simple matter of warranted prediction. Some of the warrants involve the attribution of purpose to human agents. But that is not untoward – I attribute purpose to my dog when I trust it to bark at intruders. There is nothing peculiar about trusting human beings, while trust is simply a matter of predictability.

Secondly, we trust one another to do what is right. This is more slippery, although partly because 'right' is slippery. When I lend you my copy of Kant's *Critique of Practical Reason*, I trust you to return it. I expect you to return it even though we both know that I am far too scatty to remember that you have it. In what sense exactly do I expect it? In part, no doubt, I predict that you will, since I would hardly lend the book if I thought you too careless or dishonest to rely on. But notice the moral flavour of these defects. I also expect it *of* you that you will return my copy of Kant. I am *entitled* to have it back, and you are *at fault* if you do not *oblige*. There is a bond between us and I expect you to honour it in two senses, one predictive and the other normative. On the one hand, I predict that you will. On the other, I believe that you should – or at least that you believe that you should.

These senses do not coincide. The predictive one is as before but the other injects a fresh, somewhat teasing, element. Normative expectations have what could be called a moral flavour, in that they hover uneasily between moral obligations and the local requirements of a particular society. What is expected of you is, morally, that you be trustworthy and, socially, that you abide by the relevant norms. Is this a distinction without ultimate difference? It would be, if the demands of morality were finally those of local norms or, conversely, if local norms involved obligations not accounted for by their being sanctioned by local practice. In other words, although there is a *prima facie* distinction between ethics, conceived as universal reasons for action, and ethics conceived as local reasons embodied in social norms, it is a distinction which can be contested. For the time being, however, I shall presume that the *prima facie* distinction stands but lets us speak of normative expectations under both moral and social headings.

Either way, they are not congruent with expectations which are solely of the predictive sort, as with reliable clocks and regular habits. The normative differs from the normal. One useful social skill is to have a shrewd idea how far people can be relied on to do what is expected of them. For example, officials are (usually) forbidden to take bribes. But some are bribable nevertheless and it can be useful to know whom, when and how. Yet the dividing line is not always clear-cut, since many systems would not operate if run wholly by the book. A civil service may be so badly paid that bribery within limits is officially tolerated. An organisation may work better if the chiefs connive at employees fiddling the petty cash. For such examples, a further set of entitlements and duties, together with a language of praise and blame, is in play. But although this may show ambiguity about what the real norms are or how far they extend, it does not suggest that the normative reduces to the normal. The difference will be memorably clear to anyone who reflects on the signal which Nelson sent to the fleet in 1805 at the start of the battle of Trafalgar: 'England expects every man to do his duty this day.' The signal put his trust in their patriotism and sense of duty. Since he thought his sailors the scum of the sea, he may not have expected *that* they would do their duty, at least without the help of petty officers ready to shoot those disinclined to do so; but he still expected it *of* them.

With a distinction between normal and normative in mind, I can next introduce the idea of strategic action. Max Weber defined social action as 'action which takes account of the behaviour of others and is thereby oriented in its course'.[5] Whether social action is strategic depends on the kind of account taken. For instance, I cross the road, relying on you to stop at the red light, or spot you walking across the park and set my path to intersect with yours. These are strategic choices if and only if what I expect you to do depends on what I expect you to expect me to do. When I spot you crossing the park, shout for your attention and point to a salient tree, and when you wave back and head that way, we are acting strategically. We have each recognised what the other proposed and have acted to help solve a small problem. When I cross the road and you do not stop at the light, we have not. Action is social if it takes account of the behaviour of others, and is strategic if it takes account of the account which others take.

Strategic action is basic for social life and social science. People

5. *Economy and Society*, ed. G. Roth and C. Wittich, New York: Bedminster Press, 1968, chapter 1.

could not live together without pooling their interests and coordinating their actions. Nor would their less cooperative activities be possible without taking account of the account which others take. Trust is crucial, but in which sense? For simple coordination, the obvious answer is that predictive expectations are enough. You and I want to meet; so you predict that I will go to the place where I predict that you will go, and *vice versa*. There is an inherent regress here, which will be discussed in chapter 7, but it does not sound as if it called for a sense of trust other than the predictive. Yet, to give warning, we shall find reason to invoke a normative notion of trust, whenever we consider strategic action in the context of the theory of games. Meanwhile, the starting point is that each of us predicts what the other will do, on the assumption that the other is rational. The word 'rational' needs watching and will be defined presently. For the moment, suppose that to act rationally is to act intelligently in pursuit of one's ends.

Whether there is finally a difference between the predictive and normative senses of trust is not straightforward. There is clearly some difference between my predictive expectation that you will be punctual (since you always are) and my normative expectation that you will (since courtesy demands it). The one prompts me to trust you and the other entitles me to do so. They may come together when we reflect that whether you will do as courtesy demands depends on your character and circumstances, and so on your desires and beliefs. This may suggest that the predictive sense is basic. On the other hand, normative expectations have their source in social norms and moral qualities and it can be argued that either or both make a basic difference. People do not obey norms solely out of prudence, we shall find, and reasons for action which hinge on mutual recognition of moral qualities affect the descriptions under which actions are done. To anticipate a later theme, trusting people to act in their self-interest is one thing and trusting them to live up to their obligations another. The former does not capture the bond of society, since the bond relies on trusting people not to exploit trust. That connects in turn with a dispute about the proper sense of 'rational' and of the rationality involved in strategic action. All this leaves it unclear for the moment whether expectation finally always carries a predictive sense, especially one which would unify the natural and social sciences.

THE ENLIGHTENMENT TRAIL

Even if there is an incipient problem about trust where people are rational and their interests do not coincide, nothing has yet been said to suggest a paradox. That there is one will be plainest if we now switch to the particular by taking a definition of rationality as doing what best suits one's preferences and considering what follows for ideally rational agents interacting strategically. This will then be used to embarrass the Enlightenment vision of an enlightened society where people know no other master than their reason. Even granted enlightened institutions, how will the interests of each be reconciled with the interests of all? Trust is part of the answer, but an easy part of too easy an answer which wishes away all serious conflicts of interest. I find this utterly unconvincing. The snag is not only that Condorcet's project includes engineering 'the motives that direct our feelings and actions' and I doubt both the effectiveness and the morality of that. It is also that he fails to realise that reason, as envisaged, may be an active solvent of trust, thus missing an especially teasing problem where emancipation dissolves the traditional bonds of society. It would indeed be paradoxical if the progress of reason destroys ties which free people need. That will open up the largest question of how societies can overcome conflicts of interest while accepting reason as the final guide to life. Only if it has an answer can we dispose of the rival view that trust depends on habits and virtues which defy reason.

So let us continue with the idea of strategic choice and take the makers of strategic choices to be, until further notice, the ideally rational agents of rational choice theory, who know one another to be ideally rational agents. These paragons of rationality are unlike you and me in ways which will become crucial. In particular, they do what is expected of them only if it is in their interests; and that makes it plausible to argue that laws, rules, norms and other regulators of conduct have the task of Nelson's vigilant petty officers. Rational agents act morally only when they find it rational. Without sanctions or incentives, virtue and happiness tend to pull apart, thus snapping the links in Condorcet's unbreakable chain.

If something is truly in the interests of all, it is in the interests of each Adam and Eve, Jack and Jill. If these rational agents are truly enlightened and free individuals 'who know no other master than their reason', why does each need sanctions or incentives to do what is in their interest? After all, most systems of enforcement are inconvenient, inefficient and expensive – what economists neatly term a deadweight loss. It is paradoxical, if the progress of reason makes them more necessary, rather than less. Yet ideally rational agents find themselves in a very instructive quandary. To bring this out, I shall now set a puzzle, intended to define the paradox in a formal way, and then resume the richer colours which highlight our ambivalence about reason.

The puzzle is set in a scenic wilderness, through which there runs a glorious walk, known as the Enlightenment Trail. The Trail ascends through smiling uplands and is blessed with six inns or pubs to tempt the thirsty traveller. Adam and Eve have decided to tackle it next weekend. But, being drinkers as much as walkers, they have agreed that they will stop at just one of these watering holes and that their walk will end there. As they reach each pub, they will take it in turns to decide whether to halt or to walk on, with Adam having the first turn.

The first pub is a low tavern called The Rational Choice, which neither much cares for. To be precise, Adam would give it 1 point in his ranking of 5 for the best pub and 0 for the worst, and Eve would give it 0 in hers. Scores are recorded in the bracket by each pub on the map, with Adam's rating first, then, after a comma, Eve's. The next pub is The Social Contract and it too scores low {0,2}. Then the standard rises somewhat as the trail reaches The Foole {3,1} and The Sensible Knave {2,4}. But the best pubs are clearly the final two, The Extra Trick {5,3}, which Adam puts top of his list, and The Triumph of Reason {4,5}, which both like well and Eve ranks top.

Where will their walk end? The Enlightened answer should presumably be that a pleasant stroll through the verdant landscape will

A
            * The Triumph of Reason   (4, 5)
        E
            * The Extra Trick   (5, 3)
    A
            * The Sensible Knave   (2, 4)
    E
        * The Foole   (3, 1)
A
        * The Social Contract   (0, 2)

    * The Rational Choice   (1, 0)   *The Enlightenment Trail*

bring them to The Triumph of Reason for a beaker full of the warm south in the evening sunshine. But, before drawing that conclusion, we need to be definite about how Adam and Eve tick. Suppose, without being too definite for the moment, that each is the very model of a modern individual, self-interested, rational and knowing the other to be so also. Adam is directly concerned only with how much *he* likes any particular pub and Eve is directly concerned only with how much *she* likes it. That need not make each oblivious of the other's likes and dislikes; but any such vicarious concern can take only two forms, one substantive and the other strategic. Substantively, it can affect what makes a pub desirable, for instance because Adam is fond of Eve. In that case, since his utility-rankings respond to hers, he will already have marked up any pub which she fancies (within limits, because neither could act at all if each cared only to satisfy the other's preferences). Strategically, each needs to note how the other ranks the pubs, because each needs to know what the other is likely to do. In that case, Adam will be aiming for whichever pub is his best target, allowing for Eve's similar attempt to do the best for herself; and *vice versa*. This latter element, introduced through the assumption that each knows the other to be a rational agent, makes it less plain that the Enlightenment Trail ends for them at The Triumph of Reason.

So where will it end? I am sorry to say that Adam and Eve will not make it to The Triumph of Reason. For, if they reach the final fork,

Adam will opt for The Extra Trick. But they will not get to the final fork, because Eve would stop the walk at The Sensible Knave, since she prefers it to The Extra Trick. So Adam would not give her the chance and would halt at The Foole. Eve would prefer The Social Contract, however, and, to do better than this low tavern, Adam will have to stop the walk even sooner. So his rational choice turns out to be The Rational Choice; and self-interest, even enlightened self-interest, turns out to be self-defeating. Sad, isn't it?

Or is it cheering for us less rational mortals? Before we decide, I should stress the point about pay-offs and self-interest. With the pay-offs given in pubs, Adam and Eve can seem strictly selfish. In that case the self-defeating outcome might simply serve them right. But this is not what an assumption that Adam and Eve are ideally rational agents commits us to. Ideally rational agents inhabit the world of rational choice theory and the theory of games, which I shall describe presently. Compared with the everyday world, it is both an abstraction and idealisation. It abstracts from particular desires or goods, like glasses of ale, cosy surroundings or the pleasure of someone's company, and deals in 'preferences' or 'utilities', thus introducing a universal language and agent-relative measure of value. Adam and Eve each have an order of preference for the pubs, only in part to do with the ales on offer and perhaps complicated by the other's preferences. But such specific ingredients disappear when they are expressed in an abstract language of utilities. So, apparently, does any specific story about what motivates them psychologically, apart from a general assumption that more utility is better than less. Hence, provided that the adjusted pay-offs are as stated, it makes no difference whether Adam and Eve are selfish sods or ardent altruists. The sorry outcome depends solely on assuming that Adam is directly moved only by what Adam wants overall, and Eve directly moved only by what Eve wants overall. Philosophically, the abstraction can be regarded as a way of rendering specific a very general desire/belief model of action appropriately for a technical theory of strategic choice.

Abstraction omits; idealisation adds. If Adam and Eve are less than human in their lack of particular desires and satisfactions, they are also more than human in their perfect consistency of preferences, powers of reasoning and knowledge of one another. Ideally rational agents will turn out to be very strange creatures. But, until further notice, let us regard them merely as very clear-headed and well informed versions of our everyday selves. How far their troubles stem from their being *ideally* rational will be a later topic.

PROMISES, PROMISES: NATURE'S PARADOXICAL TASK

Since Adam and Eve are not stupid, will they not escape the paradox by making an agreement? 'Tell you what,' says Adam, 'I promise to keep going, if you will promise to keep going; and I promise not to opt for The Extra Trick at the end.' 'Fine by me,' says Eve, who also prefers The Triumph of Reason to The Rational Choice, 'I promise to keep going too.' Well, yes; but does this exchange of words make any difference? Not, I suggest for the moment, unless it changes their rankings of the pubs. If Adam still prefers The Extra Trick to The Triumph of Reason, then, being a rational individual as defined, he will still opt for it, except, of course, that Eve will still not give him the chance. In short, all is as before, since, as game theorists are wont to say, words are cheap talk.

This abrupt dismissal of an obvious solution is not meant as the final word on agreements between rational agents. It is warranted at this stage by the abstraction performed in presenting Adam and Eve as rational individuals. Words are cheap talk in the sense that they matter only if they address what matters to a rational individual. So far, rational agents do only what they would have done without them. But, since the dismissal is likely to seem too abrupt, let us take the question of a rational agent's psychology more slowly.

I have introduced Adam and Eve by abstracting them directly from flesh-and-blood people with all sorts of beliefs and desires. It may be helpful to insert an intermediate stage, which engages with a common view of what this 'economic' style of thinking involves, namely a substantive claim about human nature and a straight connection of rationality to self-regarding motives. It is memorably captured by F. Y. Edgeworth's dictum that 'the first principle of economics is that every agent is actuated solely by self-interest'.[6] When this principle is combined with the standard rationality assumptions of economics, it results in an economic science predicated on self-regarding behaviour. That may be one reason why economics has sometimes been dubbed 'the dismal science'. Edgeworth is far from alone in regarding self-interest as the first principle. In that case, whether it is a sound first principle seems to depend on whether it is empirically true. Edgeworth himself thought it accurate enough for the study of commerce, although less applicable to labour markets and other areas of economic activity. Other economists have thought it true of economic behaviour at large. Other social scientists have adopted it as a fundamental truth about human behaviour, especially in politics but also in everyday social relations. For a fine example, here is a remark from Peter Blau's *Exchange and Power in Social Life:*[7]

> An apparent altruism pervades social life, people are anxious to benefit one another and to reciprocate for the benefits they receive. But beneath this seeming selflessness an underlying 'egoism' can be discovered...A basic reward people seek in their associations is social approval and selfish disregard for others makes it impossible to obtain this important reward.

If self-regarding motives were indeed a central fact of social life and hence involved in the very idea of rational agency, the problem of trust would be set by this specific claim about human psychology, if not universally then at least for specific historical conditions like our own. In that case, one response is to credit human beings, including our own neighbours, with more genial motives, thus making the prospects for unpoliced trust less dismal. Debate conducted at this level of partial abstraction from apparent altruism and other motives to a more general egoism has indeed marked the problem of trust, as we shall find in the next chapter. But the ground is tricky, because many theorists, including economists, hover between a definite psychology and a merely schematic account of motivation, compatible with varied empirical claims. For instance, Gary Becker is perhaps the best known

6. F. Y. Edgeworth, *Mathematical Psychics*, London: Kegan Paul, 1881, p. 16.

7. P. Blau, *Exchange and Power in Social Life*, New York: John Wiley, 1964, p. 17.

exponent of an 'economic' approach to human behaviour all across the board:

> Indeed I have come to the position that the economic approach is a comprehensive one that is applicable to all human behaviour, be it behaviour involving money prices or imputed shadow prices, repeated or infrequent decisions, emotional or mechanical ends, rich or poor persons, men or women, adults or children, brilliant or stupid persons, patients or therapists, businessmen or politicians, teachers or students.[8]

It leads him to make many remarks which sound like Blau's underlying egoism, as when he says, 'A person decides to marry when the utility expected from marriage exceeds that expected from remaining single or from an additional search for a more suitable mate.' Yet he also declares that 'all human behaviour can be viewed as involving participants who maximise their utility from a stable set of preferences' and this is consistent with many motives, including even genuine altruism.

At any rate, the paradox of the Enlightenment Trail emerges at a level of abstraction where the idea of rationality is divorced from speculations about human psychology, whether universal or specific. Motivation is to do solely with utilities and preferences, and is compatible with any or every substantive account of what makes people tick. Does Adam care about Eve or merely about how to exploit her preferences? Many contemporary rational choice and game theorists see no need to answer, on the grounds that the analysis of rational action involves no particular psychology of any kind, is purely formal at heart and depends solely on formal axioms of choice.

Yet that sounds too slick. Is there or is there not an assumption of egoism, which makes for tension between the interests of each and the interests of all? Well, now you see it, now you don't. Even if there is no invariable *psychological* egoism, there is still prone to be a *philosophical* egoism in all accounts of what motivates human agents. It surfaces when we ask how exactly a preference for *x* over *y*, or a calculation that *x* offers more utility than *y*, moves someone to act. In so far as prefer-

---

8. G. Becker, *The Economic Approach to Human Behavior*, University of Chicago Press, 1976, p. 8.

ences are a newer name for what used to be called passions, the classic answer is that the agent expects to gain greater psychological satisfaction. Since not all sources of satisfaction are self-centred, there is room for many desires and many ways to satisfy them. If 'self-interest' is construed in this broader sense, we can still hold that 'every agent is actuated solely by self-interest'. But what is then meant is that all action comes about as the stock desire/belief model suggests, by the prompting of desire, tempered by the agent's beliefs about alternative ways to satisfy it. Crucially, Adam is moved solely by what Adam wants and Eve solely by what Eve wants. Call this *philosophical egoism*.

Are preferences a newer name for what used to be called passions? Philosophical egoism goes with a moral psychology, to use another venerable term, and involves some psychology, however diluted. This thought has prompted a history of attempts to remove all trace of psychology from the pure theory of rational choice. To achieve it, preferences are treated not as inner states which motivate action but components of a pattern revealed by and in the choices which agents make. A rational choice becomes a choice consistent with other choices, in a pattern which can be called an order of preference. I shall return to this in the next chapter. To anticipate, however, one result is to withdraw the theory of choice from the work of explaining action. Preferences which *are* choices do not *explain* choices. Conversely, if a desire/belief model is explanatory, it needs to regard preference as an expression of desire tempered by belief. The psychology can be kept schematic, since philosophers are no experts, but it cannot be expelled altogether.

Meanwhile, even the least committal versions assume that action is guided by how the agent ranks its consequences. One can argue about what is allowed into their description, for instance whether my act of buying an Oriental carpet has a different result depending on whether the carpet was woven by sweated child labour or by consenting adults and on whether I am sensitive to this difference. But one cannot wonder whether only consequences matter, since it is assumed that whatever matters can be expressed in consequential terms. Contrasting ways of conceiving rational agents have this in common.

The assumption goes very deep, as we shall find when we consider trying to dislodge it later.

We shall also find that a presumption of individualism is deeply entrenched. Why have we been thinking of any outcome which Adam and Eve reach as the sum of a strategic choice by Adam and a strategic choice by Eve? The answer congenial to philosophical egoism is that Adam and Eve are *au fond* separate individuals, not, for example, irreducibly a couple, partnership or collective body. Each is prior to any ends which they share. Could one conceive of an egoism in the first person plural, so that your actions and mine are expressions of what *we* desire and believe? That is not self-evidently absurd. But it is not a thought usually entertained by theories of rational and strategic choice. The content of philosophical egoism is hard to pin down, since it seems to commit one to so very little. But, in practice at any rate, its 'ego' is an individual working in the first person singular.

Philosophical egoism is elusive: now you see it, now you don't. But it is involved in the presumption that action results from the desires and beliefs, from the preferences, information and processing of the (individual) agent; and that is enough to pose the problem of trust. Translated into the language of economic theory, each of us is an expected utility maximiser or, in plainer prose, a bargain-hunter. Rational Adam looks ahead to the pay-offs attaching to the consequences of his possible actions. He cannot resist the lure of a marginally higher pay-off. Nor can Eve; and the sum of their choices can be suboptimal for both of them. When they see an inferior outcome in prospect, they can try to head it off by agreeing to cooperate. But words are cheap talk since each keeps an agreement only when breaking it pays less, all things considered. So they do what they have promised only if they would have done it anyway. That is why, at this stage of the story, two ideally rational agents, setting off down the Enlightenment Trail, have as yet no hope of reaching The Triumph of Reason.

So, if we are rational individuals, how is social life possible at all? Social life depends on trust, especially on trust that promises will be kept. Yet there would be no institution of promising if we reconsid-

ered our promises whenever the moment came to honour them, and
then kept them only if we did not do better by breaking them.
Promising works only if promises are kept *just because they have been
made*. Here lies a crux, as Nietzsche indicates with a nicely pointed
question:[9]

> To breed an animal capable of promising (*das versprechen darf*) – isn't that just
> the paradoxical task which nature has set herself with mankind, the peculiar
> problem of mankind?

To be precise, the peculiar problem is to breed an animal capable of
keeping promises even on occasions when an assessment of consequences, as measured by the expected utility of their pay-offs, bids us
defect. It is posed in the first instance by presenting Adam and Eve as
characters drawn by a simplified theory of rational choice in the
service of an instrumental notion of rationality. That swiftly makes for
a paradox of trust. The stronger the bond of trust, the more a society
can progress; the more it progresses, the more rational its members
become and hence the more instrumental in their dealings with one
another; the more instrumental their relations, the less trustworthy
they are. So the progress of reason erodes the bond which made it possible and which it continues to need.

Conclusion

Since thinkers in the Enlightenment line are likely to think the
paradox spurious, I should rehearse the point of the Enlightenment
Trail. In the first instance, it sets a puzzle, well-defined within the
theory of games, where it is known as a 'centipede'. The logic which
seems to defeat a mutual interest in cooperation is known as backward
induction and the puzzle is whether it can be resisted within the standard rules of the game, at least when the game is to be played several
times. This, secondly, is not a straightforward question, partly because
there may be technicalities involved and partly because the standard
rules may not be utterly clear about the relation of rationality, prefer-

---

9. *The Genealogy of Morals* (1887), New York: Doubleday, 1956, II.1.

ence and self-interest. These provisos combine to raise a wider question about the scope and limits of rational choice theory and the theory of games. The question has several facets, among them whether the notion of practical reason embodied in 'rational agents' is an idealisation or a distortion of the one accompanying the desire/belief model of action. Thirdly, the trail raises the problem of trust in a wider Enlightenment context, as the names of the pubs indicate, to be pursued in a spirit which is partly historical and partly analytical. This wider question is the one signalled earlier as that of trust-within-reason and the pubs suggest some classic answers which we shall examine as we go. The Enlightenment Trail is thus the meeting point for the puzzle, paradox and general problem of trust, construed for the purposes of this book.

Is the paradox still spurious? Condorcet, for instance, has nature endowing us with a capacity to form ties of interest and duty, thus setting us on a path of truth, virtue and happiness where no such paradox could occur. But, even in its own terms, this waves aside awkward questions about 'the reconciliation, the identification of the interests of each with the interests of all' and I shall presume that the paradox must be taken seriously. It may still be spurious finally, however. A first thought is to try a less simplistic idea of rational and strategic choice, and a second is to recall that the underlying desire/belief model of action is, in any case, broader than any formal decision theory. Reason, instrumentally defined, has several tricks up its sleeve, as we shall see in the next two chapters. They may even include dropping the naturalism involved in supposing human nature to be a complex feature of the natural order and in modelling the moral and political sciences on the natural sciences.

Meanwhile, the crux is that Adam and Eve will not make it safely along the Enlightenment Trail and into the snug at The Triumph of Reason, unless they are 'capable of promising'. The general problem of trust is one of identifying the bond of society, of specifying what makes for a weaker or stronger bond and then of shaping institutions and policies accordingly. Does it have a solution consoling for the philosopher who laments the errors, crimes and injustices which still pollute the earth? That depends on whether the solution is within reason. So far I have offered only a loose general definition of rationality and a very artificial setting for a more precise one. The next chapter will try some ways to bring them together.

2
The perils of prudence

This chapter will tackle the modern problem of the first by giving it a historical setting while the next chapter will provide a contemporary one. But we need to start with a plan for the whole book. The next section sets out accordingly.

PLAN OF THE BOOK

The opening chapter began with recent ideas of rational action and where they are heading. Then it set them in an older context of Enlightenment hopes and fears, prompted by plausible doubts about the problem of trust. Straight ahead lies a simple treatment of rational action as the pursuit of any end in an instrumental way, with or without a further claim that questions about ends are simple too. This will fail, however, if ends are ambiguous in ways affecting their rational pursuit. There are three possibilities. The simplest is that each of us can do as we think best for ourselves, provided that we do what suits us all. But this may turn out less simple than it seems, when we reflect on the tension between the good of each and the good of all. Can the simplest idea cope with it? If not, we must accept that something more is needed. It could be, secondly, that a rational person's ends have to be moral in a sense which makes our individual concerns subordinate to those of humanity. Trust is a sign that we are rational enough to accept the point. Or it could be, thirdly, that we need thicker ends which cannot all come from further reflection on our personal advantage.

These worries could be due simply to not knowing the power of game theory to resolve what used to be snags for the idea of rational choice. But, since I do not believe this, the book is structured differently. In this chapter and the next, we shall give game theory a try, starting with attempts by Hobbes and Hume, who both saw the problem, and continuing with later attempts to do better. But it turns out that the snag was not a lack of technicalities. Indeed, modern technicalities serve to make the difficulty plain by showing how they can only presuppose what they need to assume. This emerges from reflection on Bentham's precise scheme and later attempts to do without his residual psychology. It emerges also from precise conclusions about why backward induction defeats us even when we give the problem a wider setting and allow other occasions to bear on it.

Chapters 4 and 5 try out some older alternatives, starting with Hume's 'remedy in the judgement and the understanding' and advancing by way of Adam Smith to Immanuel Kant's moral solution. That gives a historical setting for recent contractarians who equate rational agents with autonomous agents but ultimately to no effect. A moral solution is too unconditional; and neither the more austere Gauthier nor the more generous Rawls can find another stopping place. So is 'the bond of society', in Locke's phrase, a matter of our thinking collectively? Chapter 7 rejects ways of treating the thought suggested by Lewis and, with a different aim, by Schelling, and insists that we try a full-blooded shift to a collective point of view. But this requires thoughts about the primacy of a different idea of persons and perhaps of teams, as I explore first in chapter 6. We are too far into local communities for Enlightenment acceptance.

Chapter 8 therefore takes the light at the end of the Enlightenment trail as a matter of distinguishing personal reciprocity from the generalised reciprocity which Enlightenment requires. This calls for what Rousseau terms 'a remarkable change in man' and sets modern liberals a dilemma. Shall they stick to the idea that, in Condorcet's words, 'truth, virtue and happiness form an unbreakable chain' or settle for the current distinction between procedural and substantive values? The latter is is more attractive, until we notice that it does not make sense. But the former seems to let the expert social engineer dictate the truth about how we should be. The question is then whether the social engineer can be met by insisting that truth about human affairs is partly a construct. But this depends on its not being wholly one; and the story ends in a tension which it tries to resolve. Only if it succeeds can trust be finally a matter of the spread of reason and not of its limits.

That is a sketch of the book as a whole. Historically, the scientific revolution prompted a new idea of reason both in science and, less obviously or immediately, in the theory of action. Previously, when science and the Bible were in harmony as guides to the universe, reason addressed a unitary question about the cause, function, purpose and meaning of whatever was part of the order of things. Although one could distinguish between, for instance, proximate and final causes, everything belonged to a scheme which was causally complete, aesthetically elegant and morally organised. That included human beings, in so far as they exercised their free will in accord with natural law. But the revolution in science, especially in mechanics and astronomy, was creating a new picture of nature. The world was becoming like a watch, to cite a common seventeenth-century image, a perfect machine working with geometrical precision in accordance with universal laws of motion. To explain how the parts of a watch work and interact is to speak a language of causes and functions, which does not require a purpose for the watch and still less a meaning of its existence.

The severance between how and why, between scientific and moral questions, has never been wholly complete or universally accepted. But it was looming in the seventeenth century and was taking definite shape in the eighteenth. So there was trouble in store for attempts at a science of mind and for Condorcet's 'moral and political sciences' if they hoped to arrive at moral conclusions. Reason, as deployed in natural science and enshrined in the idea of theoretical reason, was losing touch with practical reason, as deployed in an understanding of human action with implications for ethics. It might be impossible to combine what is natural, rational and right. Indeed, the new moral sciences, far from forging an unbreakable chain between truth, virtue and happiness, might find themselves demonstrating that no such chain could be forged. The thinkers who will help us along the Enlightenment Trail saw the problem clearly but, each in his own way, thought it was soluble. Hobbes struck an Enlightenment note for all by remarking, *'Reason* is the *pace*; Encrease of *Science*, the *way*; and the Benefit of man- kind, the *end.'*[1]

Analytically, the problem of trust seems to me to have been fully defined by the end of the eighteenth century and the options explored. We shall try Hobbes and Hume in this chapter, Smith and Kant in chapter 5 and, with due caution about his place in an Enlightenment scheme, Rousseau in chapter 7. If none succeeds, it will be idle for Condorcet to hope for a day when the human race has no other master than its reason.

FEAR

Meanwhile, we have more immediate concerns prompted by the opening chapter. Moved by their desires and influenced by their beliefs, rational agents, as conceived so far, do what has the best consequences for themselves. Adam seeks to satisfy his desires, Eve hers. Although their desires need not be selfish, each is an egoist in the philosophical sense that other people's concerns, when more than a strategic matter, enter vicariously. Each can have a preference for satisfying other people's preferences; but Adam's preferences over Eve's preferences are still Adam's, and *vice versa*. As rational agents, they each rank actions by whether the consequences suit themselves and thus work within a frame of forward-looking, self-regarding reasons. Any seemingly joint outcome of their actions is a sum of their separate individual choices.

Let us call such rational agents prudent. That emphasises their

---

1. *Leviathan* (1651), ed. R. Tuck, Cambridge University Press, 1991, chapter V.

readiness to take an enlightened view of their interests and to choose with an eye to a more satisfying future. But it does not deny that prudence has its perils, as shown formally, if artificially, by the failure of Adam and Eve to advance past The Rational Choice. Less formally, it is also shown by everyday examples of people who are, one might say, too rational for their own good. For instance, whalers would all rather that everyone caught a limited number of whales, thus leaving enough to conserve a stock for the future, than that each caught as many as possible now. But, although this suggests the prudence of agreeing to limit catches, it notoriously fails to guarantee that anyone will abide by such an agreement. Rational choices by each can sum to an outcome inferior for all.

The obvious remedy is to introduce sanctions. Rational agents count costs among the consequences of their actions, and it can benefit everyone to raise the cost of doing what sums to an inferior outcome for all. Adam and Eve might get past The Rational Choice, if there was a penalty for failing to do what one has agreed to do. Here is a first way for them to advance prudently along the trail and, prompted by Thomas Hobbes, I shall call it 'fear'. This chapter will consider it and then try a second, 'sympathy', which is due to David Hume. Although they sound very different, they agree in making us out to be philosophical egoists and so unable to stand back from our own concerns. That is attempted by Hume himself and Adam Smith in the name of impartiality. But, even if it might be prudent to be impartial, Immanuel Kant will insist that we are now in the realm of morality and need a profoundly different idea of practical reason to ground the notion of duty.

There were thus at least four individualist accounts of human nature and practical reason on offer by the end of the eighteenth century, which can be summed up in a word each as fear, sympathy, impartiality and duty. Their authors are Hobbes, Hume, Smith and Kant; and, for anyone who denies that individualism can manage the normative sense needed for trust, there is also Rousseau. These five authors will be our guides to the Enlightenment Trail, partly for historical reasons but more because I believe them to offer all the modern options available for dealing with the problem of trust in an analytical way. If none succeeds, especially when we stress how other games influence what it is rational to do in a present one, we must concede that it is not the sleep of reason which produces monsters but reason itself.

Leviathan, published in 1651, was written in the aftermath of the English Civil War. That terrible lesson in the collapse of trust set Hobbes thinking about what it takes for rational human beings to live together in peace. The seminal chapter XIII treats 'Of the Naturall Condition of Mankind, as concerning their Felicity, and Misery'. We are essentially self-regarding, Hobbes declares, and become enemies as soon as you and I both want the same thing but cannot both have it. This basic human nature of ours gives rise to three principal causes of quarrel: competition in the face of scarcity, diffidence (distrust) of one another, and 'glory' or (roughly) an obsession with status fuelled by a belief that we are undervalued. The state of nature is therefore 'a war of everyman against everyman', where the life of man is 'solitary, poore, nasty, brutish and short'. The only escape lies in our mutually agreeing to create 'a power to keep all in awe'. This power is, as pre-saged in the Introduction, 'that great LEVIATHAN called a COMMON-WEALTH, or STATE, in Latin CIVITAS, which is but an artificial man'. Leviathan is to be armed with a monopoly of legitimate force to protect us and to enforce whatever later covenants we make with one another. For, crucially, 'Covenants, without the Sword, are but Words, and of no strength to secure a man at all' (chapter XVII). With Leviathan in place, however, peace ensues and we are free to seek 'commodious living' and the felicity of this life, which consists in a perpetual and rest-less pursuit of future goods, ceasing only in death.

Fear is the key to trust and makes it rational to subscribe to incen-tives to be trustworthy. I can trust you if and only if you dare not let me down. I realise that you can trust me only on similar terms. Since we shall both do better if we can trust one another, it suits us both to form a club, each forfeiting our own chance to do the other down, in exchange for protection from the other's aggression. The club is an association of individuals who rationally construct a power to keep all in awe, rather as the early inhabitants of the American Wild West, finding their lives nasty, brutish and short, might agree to appoint a sheriff for their mutual benefit.

Prudence thus gets Adam and Eve at least as far as The Social Contract. But such a contract looks fragile for two reasons, both of clear current concern. The first is that, if only fear keeps us honest, each member of the club will rationally break the rules whenever it is safe to do so. That will be often, even if we stiffen the policing by adding social disapproval to legal and other penalties levied on known defaulters. For, even though a rational agent will find that it pays to be of good repute, being truly honest does not always pay as well as being thought honest when one is not.

This is a serious matter in a shifting modern society, where people are opaque to one another. In Plato's version of the problem of trust, Gyges is a Lydian shepherd who finds a magic ring which can make him invisible. With its help, he makes his way into the royal palace, seduces the queen and gets her to aid him in killing the king. Gyges then becomes the new king, marrying the queen and living happily ever after. The story, prefaced by a report that many moderns are declaring society to be a contract for mutual advantage, is put to Socrates in book II of *The Republic* and the question is whether Gyges had any reason not to use the ring. This may make it seem as if the problem is one about those few master criminals strong enough to ignore morality in getting what they want. But, in today's shifting societies of partial strangers, we can all be invisible often enough. For example, suppose that you find a fat wallet in a lonely place on a dark night, containing £1,000 and the owner's name and address. If fear is the only key, it seems entirely rational to keep the money and discard the wallet, even though we shall all do better if everyone returns lost wallets to their owners than if everyone plays 'finders keepers'. Granted that policing, informal and formal alike, is both costly and inefficient, trust is too vulnerable to free-riders. This, according to some thinkers, partly explains why crime is on the increase.

Secondly, an image of a small Wild West township with a single sheriff is thoroughly misleading. Today's Leviathans have a huge state apparatus and, if Hobbes is right about human nature, the agents of the state have the same basic motives as the rest of us. They too seek their own felicity and, moreover, are armed with special power to obtain it. *Quis custodiet ipsos custodes?* If fear is the sole key, it is no surprise to find defects in the organisation of states, ranging from a self-serving lack of public zeal on the part of officials to a spectacular sleaze and corruption by those engaged in politics. For, although the state is commonly justified as a remedy for what would otherwise be a disastrous market failure and so as a public good, it gives its officers and servants a potential market in many of its activities. This market can even come to replace it. For instance, if the state fails to keep all in awe, the Mafia is ready to oblige, for a fee. (Intriguingly for the problem of trust, the Mafia's power to make a profit depends on its code of honour. What does honour in turn depend on if it too cannot be sustained solely by fear? The current tendency to think of the Mafia as a rational business enterprise leaves the question hanging.)

These remarks may seem to make too much of Hobbes' dour view of human nature, thus suggesting that trust is possible because we have some kindlier impulses. But the point is that fear of sanctions can at most make promise-keeping individually prudent, with the implication that it becomes irrational whenever we (or others) can avoid penalty. Sanctions cannot make us animals capable of promising, if that means keeping faith even when it would pay us not to. Hobbes sees this objection coming, however, and tries a bold, if tantalising, answer. In creating Leviathan, he contends, we do more than make it prudent to keep our promises. We acquire genuine obligations to the sovereign and hence, when we make promises, to one another. In chapter xiv he remarks:

> Covenants entered into by fear, in the condition of meer Nature, are obligatory. For example, if I Covenant to pay a ransome, or service for my life, to an enemy; I am bound by it. For it is a Contract, wherein one receiveth the benefit of life; the other is to receive mony, or service for it; and consequently, where no other Law (as in the condition, of meer Nature) forbiddeth the performance, the Covenant is valid. Therefore Prisoners of warre, if trusted with the payment of their Ransome, are obliged to pay it...For, whatsoever I may lawfully do without Obligation, the same may I lawfully Covenant to do through feare: and what I lawfully Covenant, I cannot lawfully break.

Really? Well, if so, that would do the trick. It would indeed make it rational for Adam, offered the final choice at the end of the Enlightenment Trail, to prefer The Triumph of Reason to The Extra Trick, thus honouring an obligation arising from a covenant with Eve to that effect.

But that is hard to accept. Even if the making of an agreement can somehow get them past The Social Contract early on, the backward induction has not been disarmed and Adam will rationally opt for The Foole. Hobbes tries to prevent this in chapter xv, where he declares it a law of nature 'that men performe their covenants made' and adds that 'in this law of Nature, consisteth the Fountain and Originall of JUSTICE.' So, once Leviathan has been created, Adam and Eve are rationally bound in justice to keep their covenants with one another. Yet Hobbes does not simply make himself a present of this easy solution. In chapter xv he also introduces a troublesome Foole:

> The Foole hath sayd in his heart, there is no such thing as Justice . . . seriously alleaging that . . . to make, or not make; keep, or not keep, Covenants was not against Reason, when it conduced to ones benefit.

The foole, Hobbes then contends, is indeed a foole, who has failed to grasp that the laws of nature are eternal and immutable, that injustice cannot be made lawful and that 'he that fulfilleth the law, is just'. The foole needs lessons in the science of the laws of nature, which is 'the true and onely Moral Philosophy. For Morall Philosophy is nothing else but the Science of what is *Good*, and *Evill*, in the conversation and Society of mankind.' The paragraph goes on to maintain that the laws of nature include '*Justice, Gratitude, Modesty, Equity, Mercy*', these being '*Morall Vertues*', and the chapter ends by saying that God has decreed them to be laws. Thus a course in moral philosophy will save Adam and Eve from making fooles of themselves.

This uplifting solution is no solution, however, or not for anyone trying to extract a modern solution from Hobbes, despite the heavy artillery thus brought to bear. In chapter xiii we were informed that in the state of nature 'nothing can be Unjust. The notions of Right and Wrong, Justice and Injustice have there no place.' Yet in chapter xiv we find that ransomed prisoners who have promised to pay up are rationally obliged to do so, thanks to the existence of a social contract which their captors were not party to; and in chapter xv this is all referred back to eternal laws decreed by God for our rational guidance as revealed by moral philosophy or science.

In upshot Hobbes seems to have reversed the line for which he is famous. His current influence in social theory stems from chapters I to xiii, as a modern thinker who starts from individualist premises, realises that individually rational choices can sum to collectively irrational outcomes and argues that the problem of public goods and free-riders is soluble if, and only if, there is a political sovereign with the power to keep all in awe. He seemed to offer either to dispense with moral obligation as the basis of trust or to ground obligation squarely in rational self-interest. Yet he then tries to deliver the genuine moral article by invoking God as a joker. If the foole's case can be answered only by invoking eternal laws and divinely ordained principles of justice, a modernised theory of obligation as self-interest mediated by contract is in trouble. The foole then has an excellent case for saying that breaking covenants is not against reason when it conduces to one's benefit.

In saying this, I mean neither to pronounce on the right way to read *Leviathan* nor, for the moment, to scotch the very idea of grounding morality in a contract. My aim is only to extract a shrewd modern posing of the problem of trust, together with a sharp query for any solution which appeals to reason by invoking sanctions. Whatever his other affiliations, Hobbes is an early architect of the Enlightenment project. The opening chapters of *Leviathan* strongly suggest that reason recommends a science of moral philosophy which identifies us as rational, self-interested beings and helps each of us serve our interests. It helps, in particular, by pointing out that, since, if left to ourselves in a state of nature, we shall each do what sums to frustrate the interests of all, we need a power to keep us all in awe. In creating Leviathan, however, we do not transmute human nature; and his later recourse to God and eternal laws, with echoes of the natural law tradition, seem to me not to affect his starting point and opening moves.

In any case, the initial line is what matters for Hobbes' place as founder of a thoroughly modern science of rational action. He firmly suggests that action is rational if it is effective in satisfying the agent's desires, as endorsed by practical reasoning addressed to the consequences of alternative actions. Covenants are rational ways to secure mutual benefits, provided that they are backed by sanctions. Can practical reason, so construed, guide Adam and Eve past The Social Contract without landing them at The Foole, instead of reaching The Triumph of Reason? The immediate crux is whether covenants without the sword are indeed but words. Hobbes' social contract creates the state and gives it an ultimate monopoly of legitimate power, the threat of which makes it rational for you and me to honour our promises to one another. But there's the rub. This account of obligation and the virtues of trustworthiness is strictly instrumental (if one sets aside reference to God and eternal laws), thus making it rational to default whenever self-interest is better served. Hobbes sportingly licenses the foole to point this out and thus score a persisting objection. Since there are plenty of occasions when fear does not suffice, and since no congenital bargain-hunter can resist a bargain, the approach is enjoyably self-defeating. If this is the pace which reason prescribes, then the increase of a science of strategic choice bodes ill for the benefit of mankind.

Adam and Eve are stuck at The Foole, because they cannot count on each other to honour what Hobbes calls 'covenants of mutual trust'. The covenant needed for the Enlightenment Trail is especially vulnerable, because it involves delayed performance. Eve is to promise not to stop at The Sensible Knave, in return for Adam's promise not to stop later at The Extra Trick. But, by the time they get that far, she will have done her bit and there will be nothing in his utilities to make him do his. So it would be contrary to reason for her to pass up The Sensible Knave, which she likes better than The Extra Trick.

Hobbes puts the point with his usual sharpness. In the absence of a common power to keep the parties in awe, he says in chapter xiv of *Leviathan*, covenants of mutual trust are void:

For he that performeth first, has no assurance the other will perform after; because the bonds of words are too weak to bridle men's ambition, avarice, anger, and other passions.

On the other hand, where there is a common power, he adds, such covenants are not void. But we have refused to agree, in so far as fear is what makes it rational to abide by rules stemming from the common power. Mutual trust requires a wider compliance than fear of sanctions can excite or warrant.

Yet that cannot be a general *nolle prosequi*. It must surely be the wrong gloss on Condorcet's too swift assurance that between us and our fellow creatures there are 'ties of interest and of duty, to which nature has wished to attach the most precious portion of our happiness and the most painful of our ills'. The Triumph of Reason still beckons Adam and Eve and all children of the Enlightenment. The bar is open, the snuggery snug, the view consoling to the philosopher and the company congenial to all free-thinking men and women who know no other master than their reason. We simply need another way to bind truth, virtue and happiness with an unbreakable chain. Rational agents must be either less self-interested or less foolish. What adjustment shall we make, if reason is not to fail where common sense so often succeeds?

SYMPATHY

Perhaps Adam and Eve should be more prudent about the company they keep. If Hobbesian individuals are too nasty for their own good, it serves them right that they cannot trust one another enough to cooperate. But why settle for Hobbes' account of human nature? David Hume offers an alternative which blends self-love with kindlier passions, notably sympathy or fellow-feeling. That may allow prudence to advise cooperation and will at least introduce further thoughts on practical reason.

Like Hobbes, Hume takes human nature to be universal, constant and basic for both science and ethics. But his eighteenth-century view of our motivating moral sentiments yields a wider and more genial list of passions, notably a natural sympathy for our fellows. Our basic self-love is tempered with an equally basic streak of fellow-feeling. Sometimes he writes as if self-love and sympathy were the only basic passions; sometimes he amplifies them, as in this splendid passage, penned in lapidary mood, as he gazes over all human history from his study in eighteenth-century Edinburgh:

> It is universally acknowledged that there is a great uniformity among the actions of men, in all nations and ages, and that human nature remains still the same, in its principles and operations. The same motives produce the same actions: The same events follow from the same causes. Ambition, avarice, self-love, vanity, friendship, generosity, public spirit: these passions, mixed in various degrees, and distributed through society, have been, from the beginning of the world, and still are, the source of all actions and enterprises, which have ever been observed among mankind. Would you know the sentiments, inclinations and course of life of the Greeks and Romans? Study well the temper and actions of the French and English: You cannot be much mistaken in transferring to the former most of the observations which you have made with regard to the latter. Mankind are so much the same, in all times and places, that history informs us of nothing new or strange in this particular.[2]

He thus commits himself squarely to a human nature which is constant in its principles and operations throughout history. Like Hobbes too, he proposes to make it the bedrock of a human science with practical implications. That at once raises a question, which will concern us later. The modern French and English may have the same passions as the ancient Greeks and Romans but they do not behave in the same way. If that is because the passions are differently mixed in different places and times, what governs the mixture? Since human nature is constant, variations are presumably due to social context. This suggests a social factor, independent of psychology and crucial for explaining, for instance, national character and social change. Furthermore, once a social factor obtrudes, one suspects that it is also at work in the list of passions. Can avarice be innate and merely activated by social context or is it a passion which needs a context for its

---

2. *Enquiry Concerning Human Understanding* (1748), ed. P. H. Nidditch, Oxford: Clarendon Press, 1975, VIII.I.65.

description and very existence? Are babies really all born with (the same) incipient public spirit? Formally, the answer could still be yes, coupled with an evolutionary story about how culture grows and is transmitted. But the question opens a doubt about the priority of the psychological over the social.

The doubt is not stilled by reverting to the shorter and more basic list of motivating passions. Self-love and sympathy also vary in their proportions and, one could argue, their content or meaning. At least some of this variation goes with cultural differences. That sets the stage for an argument between nature and nurture, which I shall not pursue now. But it is worth noting how it throws doubt too on Hume's assumption that the truth of the matter depends on observation. If history informs us of nothing new or strange, it is because we read history in the light of this assumption. When challenged, we have to defend it on metaphysical grounds, since it would be circular to appeal to facts which depend on it. A universal human nature owes more to metaphysics than to observation.

Meanwhile, if trust eludes ambition, avarice, self-love and vanity (roughly the Hobbesian motives), it is explained only in part by adding friendship, generosity and public spirit. To make trust rationally poss-ible, we need to dig deeper by asking how passions relate to action in general and then whether the problem set by self-regarding passions is of a sort to be overcome by invoking other-regarding ones.

Hume here takes passions to be the motivating causes of action. Reason has a part to play but only in advising us on the likely results of acting on a passion. 'Reason alone cannot be a motive to any action of the will. . .Reason is and ought only to be the slave of the passions, and can never pretend to any other office than to serve and obey them.'[3] The effect of its advice is to make particular passions blow hotter or colder in the circumstances, thus changing the overall motivation and so, sometimes, the action of the will. The process is mechanical, in that there is no self to intervene between motivation and action, and

3. A *Treatise of Human Nature* (1739), ed. P. H. Nidditch, Oxford: Clarendon Press, 1978, Book II, Part III, section 3.

reason can operate only by tempering passions which are already present. Even allowing for what Hume says about causation being a matter of correlation rather than production and about the role of imagination in influencing what we expect to happen, there is no other way for action to occur.

Although this sounds like crude eighteenth-century psychology, it can be taken in other ways. To render it philosophical, we can invoke the familiar language of a desire/belief model of action, which splits practical reason between desire and belief. The thesis is then simply that only desire can motivate, with belief advising on likely consequences. It can also be rendered as the standard 'economic' model of action, with passions translated as preferences and reason as information plus calculation. Hume, in offering a philosophical rather than psychological egoism, sets out an analysis of action which remains very widely accepted. But, being as powerful as it is neat, it restricts how we can construe the suggestion that natural sympathy will get Adam and Eve past The Foole. If that is the answer, then the utility numbers in the original diagram were wrongly stated. Initially the numbers may have seemed simply to register how each player ranked the pubs, leaving other things unconsidered. But, properly construed, they were to be read as homogenised utility numbers all along, with scope for vicarious elements like sympathies. If Adam is to pass up The Extra Trick, then it cannot be true that he prefers the utility of stopping there to the utility of halting at The Triumph of Reason.

This restriction may be negotiable, when we discuss prudence in chapter 4 with a fresh account of action. But it is implied by the initial story of practical reason. Hume credits human beings with passions which counter self-love and this might explain why we are rational to trust one another on some occasions when a Hobbesian story makes it irrational. But it does not explain how Adam and Eve can get beyond The Foole, if the original diagram states their preferences correctly with all things considered. Philosophically, passions which make for cooperation work in the same way as all others, by causing the agent to act so as to satisfy them. They do not make Adam and Eve more trustworthy on occasions when trust depends on each believing that the other will act contrary to a correctly stated balance of satisfactions. If reason only serves passions and only passions motivate, rational agents will entertain no such beliefs, because they know that rational agents never act contrary to their utility functions.

Hume sees this. He realises as clearly as Hobbes that there is a problem about trust and that it persists even if we have some kindlier motives than Hobbes allows. Here is his beautifully focused example:

> Your corn is ripe today; mine will be so tomorrow. 'Tis profitable for us both that I shou'd labour with you today, and that you shou'd aid me tomorrow. I have no kindness for you, and know that you have as little for me. I will not, therefore, take any pains on your account; and should I labour with you on my account, I know I shou'd be disappointed, and that I shou'd in vain depend upon your gratitude. Here then I leave you to labour alone: You treat me in the same manner. The seasons change; and both of us lose our harvests for want of mutual confidence and security.[4]

Translating the implicit assumptions about utilities into game-theoretic form, the crux looks like this:

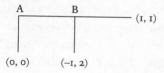

What is it rational for B to do, if the game gets that far? Rational agents, as defined earlier, are bargain-hunters and never prefer less to more. So, when tomorrow comes, B will refuse to help A, since this yields a utility of 2 (all things considered), whereas helping yields only 1. A, foreseeing this and preferring 0 to −1, will not help B today. The interests of each sum to defeat their common interest and both lose their harvests for want of mutual confidence and security.

The injection of fellow-feeling in general, and friendship, generosity and public spirit in particular, may make it prudent to trust more people than we would, if we knew everyone to be a psychological egoist. But this is trust in the first sense given earlier, that of trusting

4. *Treatise*, book III, part II, section 5.

them to be as reliable as a trusted clock. It does not cover the normative sense, in which we trust people to do what is expected of them even when that would go against their balance of satisfactions. Interestingly, Hume himself is fully aware of this and believes that societies cannot function, unless people can and do override their natural inclinations. His reason is striking too. Even our more amiable passions display a 'partiality' towards ourselves, he remarks, being kindled by people and concerns near and dear to us. We naturally favour our family over mere neighbours, for example, our friends over strangers and our compatriots over foreigners. Our natural passions do not incline us to act impartially between our own circle and other people, or, within our acquaintance, between those nearer and further from us in relationship or regard. This general propensity carries over to what he terms the 'natural virtues' and is a feature of our 'natural morality'.

Yet societies work only if people sometimes behave impartially. That is why we have rules of property and justice. The demands of justice are sternly impartial between you and me, between ours and theirs. Justice is thus an 'artificial virtue', however, and obedience to its demands requires 'a remedy, in the judgement and understanding, for what is irregular and incommodious in the affections' (*Treatise*, book III, part II, section 2). Sympathy, in short, is not enough to overcome the problem of trust. He is right, I think. But, before pursuing the problem into the realms of artifice, we must spend a further and more technical chapter on prudence.

Conclusion

Nothing in the present chapter has killed off the very idea of rational agents who reflect on what each would find rational in a world where other people lacked powers of reflection and then make corrections because their own world is one of rational agents. But this line of thought is closed to the simpler agents introduced so far. For simple rational agents, trust sets a problem not soluble within reason. They can trust others who are not guided solely by reason, although such others would be unwise to trust them in return. But trust between rational agents who know one another to be rational agents is, so far, impossible. To add motives of sympathy can make this awkward less often. But it does so by changing the utilities because those of sympathetic people differ from those of psychological egoists. It does nothing to help philosophical egoists, even sympathetic ones, on their way. Nor, as will become plain in the next chapter, does making it explicit that a single encounter may look sharper than a run of them, including those where reputations acquired in playing with one person have wider effects. That requires a different sort of agent, not merely a more stable setting.

3
The centipede's sting

In Condorcet's vision, the moral and political sciences will advance partly by learning more of how human beings tick and partly by developing a technical and precise 'social mathematics'. The unity of this enterprise depends on human nature and social mathematics being made for one another – an assumption challenged by the problem of trust. His current heirs commonly put their faith in a theory of expected utility, which encapsulates a schematic, universal account of human nature in a way suited to a theory of rational choice, including game theory, in all its elegant technicality and precision. For the purposes of this book, that means being clear what is involved, when prudence bids us make strategic choices as game theory recommends. The last chapter left some loose ends by being vague about the notion of utility and so about instrumental rationality. This one will tidy up by defining these notions more exactly and relating them to the assumptions of game theory. Whether prudence can advise us to be trustworthy depends in part on the game-theoretic implications of being prudent. Meanwhile, we are still looking for a defensible definition of reason which makes it rational to trust rational people.

Let us start with the idea of instrumental rationality. The broad idea so far has been that action is the product of the agent's beliefs and desires, and is directed to securing what the agent most wants, all things considered. Practical reasoning arrives at a rational choice of an action, or course of action, by comparing alternatives to see how completely they are likely to secure what the agent wants. This broad idea commands the assent of those who subscribe to the usual desire/belief model, I presume, at least if desire is made the sole motor. But, although clear and definite in some ways, it is ambiguous in others. What is clear can best be marked by defining an ideally rational agent with the aid of rational choice theory and game theory. Admittedly, these theories are ideal-types; and we should be wary of assuming that ideal-types are as helpful in social analysis as in the natural sciences. Rational agents, abstracted from social life and idealised, may turn out to be a source of the problem which they are supposed to illuminate. But they bring a welcome clarity to a tricky subject.

Ideally rational agents have three basic attributes: perfect information, fully ordered preferences and faultless computing:

(i) *Perfect information*: in the limiting case, Adam would hold true beliefs on all relevant matters and know them to be true. But, since this would rule out rational action done from false belief, 'perfect information' is usually taken to mean that his beliefs are consistent and have the warrant of proof or evidence, as appropriate. This is deliberately vague about the demands of epistemology. For instance, it is neutral on whether knowledge must rest on self-evident foundations or can do without them, and neutral between rationalism, empiricism, pragmatism, coherentism, reliablism and other theories of knowledge. But on two points it is definite. The first is that Adam has a 'subjective probability distribution' over the possible consequences of his actions. This is to assimilate inductive uncertainty to calculable risk and licenses the standard account of how rational agents calculate the 'expected utility' of an action. They do it by discounting the utility of its consequences by their probability, as if at roulette. Although philosophers might wish to query the assimilation of uncertainty to risk in general, it will not trouble us here.

But we should be wary of a regress arising when the probability of a consequence depends on how probable other agents think it, whenever this signals a strategic element in *everyone's* calculations. When two rational agents engage, each knows the other to be a rational agent. Each has true (or at least rational) beliefs about the other's beliefs and can perform whatever inferences the other can perform. In the ideal-type or limiting case each knows whatever the other knows. This 'common knowledge of rationality' is a curious condition, if one believes that real people are necessarily somewhat opaque to one another, and one can wonder whether it is even coherent. But it is plausible enough as a way of isolating the strategic element in games played by rational agents.

(ii) Fully ordered preferences: the ideally rational agent's preferences are complete and consistent. Eve can rank all possible consequences of her every action. She is never undecided because faced with incommensurable alternatives. For every pair of consequences, $\{xy\}$, she prefers x to y, or y to x or is indifferent between them; for every triplet $\{xyz\}$, she never prefers x to y, y to z, and z to x. This says nothing ultimate about the rationality of her ends or about whether her preferences are, for instance, kindly, sociable, virtuous, honourable or moral. It does not insist that her preferences are prompted by any particular passion or, indeed, by any passions at all. But it does leave room for a more reflective ordering than brute consistency. If we were to insist, for example, that an alcoholic could not rationally value alcohol above all else in life, rational choice theory could accommodate us up to a point by requiring that complete and consistent preferences are those affirmed after thorough reflection on the price of each in the frustration of others. But it would refuse to step outside the agent's existing motivations altogether. Call that 'reflective consistency', while noting that it needs a more complex agent than the basic model presents.

(iii) Faultless computing need not detain us. It would be an implausible condition, if taken to imply that any of us are wizards at complex

calculation. Objections have been raised on this score, when experiments show that people do not act as the model predicts. For instance, it is claimed that real people cannot manage calculations involving more than five or six steps, when working out what another player would do if. . .But the model is an idealisation; and, in any case, this point does not arise for the Enlightenment Trail, since Adam and Eve are stuck not because calculation is too complex but because it is all too simple. Meanwhile, the condition specifying faultless computing is not sabotaged by uncertainties of life or fuzziness of our preferences. With uncertainty assimilated to risk and fuzziness tidied up, after excluding incommensurability, as indifference between alternatives, we can focus clearly on the problem of trust.

In these ways the definition of a rational agent is clear, as far as it goes. But there is an ambivalence about whether rational agents have an attendant moral psychology and are motivated in any particular way. Historically, there have been three views, each a source of continuing dispute and all contributing to confusion about the role played by the concept of utility in making trust problematic, even paradoxical, for rational agents.

THREE VIEWS ABOUT MORAL PSYCHOLOGY

The first view rests practical reasoning on substantive propositions about human nature and human psychology, as with Hobbes and Hume. These propositions are universal, in that human nature is essentially the same at all places and times, even if surrounding contingencies make for individual and social differences. Thus Hobbes holds that our nature makes us enemies whenever goods are in short supply, and that we quarrel specifically because we are competitive, distrustful and glory-seeking. Hence we shall do what will sum to defeat our individual ends, unless we institute a common power to keep us all in awe. But there must be contingent factors at work too, since people and societies plainly vary. (He leaves the line between essential human passions and those dependent on social conditions or the possession of particular concepts mysterious.) Hume gives more than one list of the essential passions and, besides, says that the mixture is variable. His account of reason as the slave of the passions does not guarantee that inner or outer conflicts can always be reconciled. But neither such indeterminacies nor his scepticism about reason as traditionally conceived stop him intending the *Treatise* as the foundation for a new science of mind. Other Enlightenment thinkers assume that human nature is universal not only in its essentials and in its powers of practical reasoning but also in its moral capacities. This is the basis of new moral and political sciences to lead us along a path of truth, virtue and happiness.

I take this first view to include everyone who holds that the human sciences can rely on a moral psychology inherent in a universal human nature – an approach which remains very much alive. It thus includes Jeremy Bentham and others who hold the second view, which I take to be a contentious gloss on the first. The second view supplies a guarantee that reason can reconcile the passions and thus paves the way for rational choice theory and the theory of games. Bentham is its clearest early exponent. *An Introduction to the Principles of Morals and Legislation*[1] opens thus:

> 1. Nature has placed mankind under the governance of two sovereign masters, *pain* and *pleasure*. It is for them alone to point out what we ought to do, as well as to determine what we shall do...

Having tamed the passions by making them all sources of pain and pleasure, he can introduce a single measure of their usefulness and a principle to guide action accordingly:

> 2. By the principle of utility is meant that principle which approves or disapproves of every action whatsoever, according to the tendency which it appears to have to augment or diminish the happiness of the party whose interest is in question...
>
> 3. By utility is meant that property in any object, whereby it tends to produce benefit, advantage, pleasure, good or happiness, (all this in the present case comes to the same thing) or (what again comes to the same thing) to prevent the happening of mischief, pain, evil, or unhappiness to the party whose interest is considered: if that party be the community in general, then the

---

1. 1789, or London: Athlone Press, 1970, chapter 1.

happiness of the community: if a particular individual, then the happiness of that individual.

In a spirit akin to Condorcet's, Bentham goes on to propose a 'felicific calculus', working in 'utils'. In theory, utils were the units of a flow of psychological satisfaction or, so to speak, micro-watts of inner glow. But, witness the passage just quoted, that seems a pipe dream. Did he really suppose that there are units in terms of which 'benefit, advantage, pleasure, good or happiness' all come to the same thing? Yes, I suppose that he did, since otherwise the felicific calculus cannot always point out what we should do.

His successors soon developed doubts. For instance, J. S. Mill drew a distinction between 'lower pleasures', which bring mere contentment, and 'higher pleasures', which are the goal of a developed human being: 'It is better to be a human being dissatisfied than a pig satisfied; better to be Socrates dissatisfied than a fool satisfied.'[2] This restores a threat of incommensurability. Mill himself tried to parry it by holding that the superiority of the higher pleasures can be ascertained by asking those who have sampled both kinds: 'And if the fool, or the pig, are of a different opinion, it is because they only know their own side of the question. The other party to the comparison knows both sides.' Some economists believed him, or else settled for confining economics to what seemed more quantifiable – what Jevons termed 'the lowest rank of feeling'.[3] But this was not to abandon hope of a unified moral science, even if it set a query over its scope.

The second view is an unfinished attempt to pitch the first at a higher level of abstraction, although still one where a universal human nature and its moral psychology supply a real motivating force. 'Utility' refers to a psychological consequence of action, as well as a measure of that satisfaction and a guide for practical reasoning. The aim is a comprehensive theory of rational choice, including a solution to the problem of trust-within-reason. But the snag threatens to be

2. *Utilitarianism* (1861), Everyman edition, London: J. M. Dent & Sons, 1972, chapter 2.
3. W. S. Jevons, *The Theory of Political Economy* (1871), Harmondsworth: Penguin Books, 1970, p. 93.

that Adam and Eve are rationally capable of promising, only if they can act rationally in a way contrary to utility numbers which take everything into account. That unsettles Benthamite hopes that a felicific calculus can reduce apparent paradoxes to technical matters of rational strategic choice. So, while some economists and game theorists remain willing to have a go, others have preferred to avoid these tricky waters.

The third view, accordingly, is that a substantive moral psychology is a mistake. It attempts to fade out psychic flows, until all psychology disappears and only a logic of fully ordered preferences remains. Historically, it was pioneered by Pareto, who argued that a consumer's preferences could be represented by a map made up of 'indifference curves' or, so to speak, contour lines connecting bundles of goods between which the consumer is indifferent. Since to be indifferent between two bundles is to be just willing to exchange one for the other, nothing needs to be said about desire or pleasure. Granted that consumers always choose bundles on a higher contour line, we can describe them as utility-maximising; but this is only to say that they choose in accordance with a given set of preferences. Summing up, Pareto claimed that 'The theory of economic science thus acquires the rigour of rational mechanics; it deduces its results from experience, without bringing in any metaphysical entity.'[4]

A 'rational mechanics' has proved an attractive goal. Ramsey argued that subjective probabilities can be derived from axioms about choice between gambles.[5] Samuelson contributed a theory of 'revealed preference', in which consumer theory is derived from a compact set of axioms defining consistent behaviour in situations of choice.[6] Von Neumann and Morgenstern extended Pareto's approach to choice in the face of risk, showing that, if probabilities were

4. Vilfredo Pareto, *Manual of Political Economy* (1927), trans. A. S. Schweir. London: Macmillan, 1972, p. 113. For this paragraph and the next two, I am indebted to Robert Sugden. See M. Hollis and R. Sugden, 'Rationality in action', *Mind*, 102 (1993), pp. 5–7.

5. Frank Ramsey, 'Truth and probability', in his *The Foundations of Mathematics and Other Logical Essays*, London: Routledge and Kegan Paul, 1931.

6. Paul Samuelson, *Foundations of Economic Analysis*, Cambridge, Mass.: Harvard University Press, 1947.

known, expected utility theory could be derived from axioms about preferences.[7]

Leonard Savage rounded up these contributions and presented a quasi-logical analysis of choice under uncertainty, which he saw as an attempt to 'extend' the principles of logic 'by principles as acceptable as those of logic itself, to bear more fully on uncertainty.'[8] In a rational mechanics rationality is understood extensionally, in terms of the consistency of decisions with one another. Savage argued that someone whose preferences satisfy a suitably constructed set of postulates will choose *as if* maximising expected utility. The idea is to treat choosing as equivalent to betting on possible states of the world, grouped into alternative events, like a coin falling heads or tails. Each possible event can be assigned a number between 1 and 0, corresponding to the agent's subjective distribution of probabilities. This number can then be modified by reference to the agent's preference ranking of the events, as displayed in a willingness to gamble on their occurring. Someone whose gambles show such dispositional consistency behaves just like an agent who modifies utilities by probabilities so as to maximise expected utility.

This quasi-logical *tour de force* retains a utilitarian mathematics, while dispensing with all utilitarian psychology. What Edgeworth elegantly dubbed 'mathematical psychics' keeps its mathematics, while losing its psychics. It may seem of no relevance to the Enlightenment Trail, because the result no longer pretends to explain or justify choices by exhibiting their rationality. Instead, the meaning of psychological terms is given extensionally by reference to consistency in decisions made. Desires and beliefs thus seem to drop out, along with the broadly Humean theory of practical reason on which mathematical psychics previously relied. The notion of utility is bleached of all psychological content and we are left with an abstract scheme of quasi-logical relations. The upshot is no longer a theory of instrumental rationality, or, indeed, in the absence of all goals, ends,

7. J. von Neumann and O. Morgenstern, *Theory of Games and Economic Behavior*, 2nd edition, Princeton University Press, 1947.

8. Leonard Savage, *The Foundations of Statistics*, New York: John Wiley, 1954, p. 6.

purposes, values, aims or desires, a theory of rationality of any sort. Rationality has been transmuted into behavioural consistency. It is a behaviourist exercise which finds favour with many, but not all, game theorists.

It remains relevant, however, as a limiting case to contrast with the substantive psychology assumed initially. Whereas passions have meat in them, revealed preferences are merely schematic. Passions explain choices in the sense that we can identify (most) actions independently of particular passions, which can then be cited to account for the choice. (Adam sent Eve a bunch of roses. Why? Because he loved her.) Revealed preferences, scheduled solely by reading them off observed choices with the aid of a consistency requirement, explain nothing. (Adam's roses can be fitted in with whatever else he does, by reference to 'preferences' so constructed as to ensure it.) The limiting case replaces passions with an implicit procedural routine to ensure behavioural consistency. Admittedly, we can ask whether this limiting case is even intelligible, if truly free of all psychology. When an agent is said to behave *as if* maximising expected utility, is this *'as if'* intelligible without reference to the psychology allegedly pensioned off? But, since now is not the moment to debate whether behaviourism makes sense, we can think of the limiting case as an extrapolation from progressive attempts to reduce substantive psychological content. It is like the notional terminus of an asymptotic curve or infinite series.

The relevance is to put pressure on the idea of utility and the threefold task assigned to it in Benthamite thinking as a motivating psychological state, as a measure of satisfaction and as a principle of action. On the one hand Bentham's felicific calculus embodies a substantive claim that action results in an inner satisfaction which can be measured in utils. Alternative actions can thus be compared and the principle of action (covering both 'what we shall do' and 'what we ought to do') is to maximise utility. On the other hand, action needs a cause *a tergo* and that can only be a passion, as distinct from a generalised desire for utility, and this grants the first step towards a procedural account of what makes action rational. Hence the difference between 'preferences' and 'revealed preferences' is not as clear as it seems, when the former are thought of as inner and the latter as outer. Preferences, if conceived as distinct from passions, cannot motivate. But, unless they can, the guarantee that our motives can be represented by a consistent utility map is empty.

If Savage's rational mechanics is so schematic or purely procedural that it does not count as a theory of rationality, the reason lies finally in the idea of utility itself. Passions get converted into ghosts of passions at the moment when Bentham speaks of pleasure and pain as our two sovereign masters in the opening sentence of *An Introduction to the Principles of Morals and Legislation*. These ghosts cannot truly fill the vacuum created by treating utility as a psychological consequence of actions which it is also supposed somehow to motivate. But they haunt the theory effectively enough to hide the vacuum. Compare Leibniz's seventeenth-century way of putting a refusal to believe that a (physical) vacuum was possible. Faced with evidence that the newly invented air pump could easily create one, he retorted that every apparent vacuum was full of 'the effluvia of light and other very thin fluids'. The theory of utility, it seems to me, relies on the effluvia of very thin passions.

Preferences are thus uneasily poised between passions and procedures; and the question is whether that is a stable position. They enter the story as the search for a wholly general theory of rational action advances. Hobbes and Hume specified the passions which move us and added causal accounts of how they prompt us to do what we expect to satisfy them. But these passions were too specific to particular times and places for a universal theory which needs no help from history. So Bentham's reduction of motivating passions to pleasure and pain, with rational agents as pleasure-maximisers, seems an advance. Pleasure is glossed as 'benefit, advantage, pleasure, good or happiness', which all 'comes to the same thing', and treated as a psychological pay-off caused in the agent by the consequences of action. In so far as there is a psychological currency in which they do indeed come to the same thing, he is in the traditional business of propounding a substantive theory of human nature, uniform in its elements and universal in its application. In so far as the psychology not only transmutes all particular and perhaps merely local motivators into a fully universal scheme but also ensures commensurability, he has made progress. At any rate, he has opened the way to an ideal-type theory of rational action with an idealised psychology, expressed in the proposition that a rational agent has complete and consistent preferences.

Yet this is still too smooth. When we ask what instrumentally rational action maximises, current replies start with 'utility' and, if pressed, range from 'self-interest', through 'the overall satisfaction of the agent's desires', to 'the value of a variable in the utilitarian calculus'. Somewhere in the range there is supposedly a point where substantive and procedural elements combine to allow an instrumentally rational agent an optimal choice between actions. 'Utility' marks the spot, if there is one. The problem of trust makes it dubious. Trust apparently involves relying on others sometimes to act contrary to the balance of their expected utility, with trustworthiness a matter of willingness so to act. The model of rational action appears to make that impossible for rational agents. This difficulty is inherent in the concept of utility and not by-passed by smooth talk of preferences.

The formidable character of rational choice and game theory make it easy to regard the problem as a technical one. Since I do not, however, I shall next try to show why there is more to it. The aim is not to rebut the work of game theorists far better equipped than I to draw technical conclusions, but to argue that there are prior questions which technicalities do not dispose of.

CENTIPEDES AND BACKWARD INDUCTION

In game theory terms, the Enlightenment Trail poses the riddle of backward induction in the form of a 'centipede', so called for the resemblance which an extended version has to that insect. The core puzzle is how Hume's farmers, if rational, can cooperate to get both their harvests in. The Enlightenment Trail is an extended version with five legs. It makes no difference how many legs there are, since the logic of backward induction starts with the choice at the final node and works its way back to the first node regardless. Provided that the utility numbers rise in a suitably one-step-back-and-two-steps-forward manner, the player with the opening choice is paralysed, like the centipede in the fable when asked which leg it moved first.

For the sake of generality, here is a fresh example. Imagine that there is a heap of coins on the table in front of Adam and Eve, a gift from a good fairy, as rewards in a small game which they are about to play. Each in turn may take one coin or two. When one coin is taken, the turn passes to the other player. But as soon as either takes two coins *the game stops and the remaining coins vanish.* Adam and Eve are rational agents, who each know the other to be such. Adam has the opening turn. Will he take one coin or two?[9]

To focus the question, now suppose that there are exactly six coins on the table, as in the diagram below. The players take it in turns to advance from left to right, for as long as each player takes one coin. As soon as someone takes two, the game ends and its result is given by the numbers in brackets at the bottom of that leg. The diagram shows the total number of coins gained by each for each possible outcome of the game. Thus if Adam opens by taking two coins the game ends at once with an outcome of (2,0). If it goes full length, the outcome is (3,3), unless Adam takes two coins at his final turn, with a result of (4,2). (The pay-offs are not really in coins but in utils, utilities or measures of preference for outcomes which take all sources of satisfaction into account, as on the Enlightenment Trail; but assume this not to make a difference for the moment.) Granted that Adam is sure to prefer (4,2) to (3,3), backward induction then lands him with a best choice of (2,0). Ridiculous!

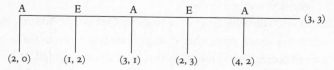

The coin game

9. For a fuller discussion, see my 'Penny pinching and backward induction', *Journal of Philosophy*, 88, (1991), pp. 473–88. This article is a rejoinder to Philip Pettit and Robert Sugden's 'The backward induction paradox', *Journal of Philosophy*, 86 (1989), pp. 169–82. See also Robert Sugden's 'Inductive reasoning in repeated games', in R. Selten (ed.), *Rational Interaction: Essays in Honor of John C. Harsanyi*, Berlin: Springer-Verlag, 1992, pp. 201–21, and Hollis and Sugden, 'Rationality in action'.

Is backward induction a valid form of reasoning? The idea for the coin game is that if there are ever just two coins left, the next player is sure to take them both. So, if there are ever just three coins left at Adam's turn, he will take two and kill the game, since otherwise he takes one and does not get another chance. So, if there are just four coins left, he will again take two, because taking one would leave three and Eve will take two of them, killing the game; and so on, whatever the precise number on the table at the start of the game. To put it another way, a game for three coins has a game for two coins embedded within it; so a rational agent opens by taking two; a game for four coins has a game for three coins embedded within it; and so on. Hence the argument holds, whatever precise size of game we consider. So a rational agent kills a six-coin game at the start, with a result of (2,0), even though (4,2) would have been better for both and (3,3) not only better but also fairer. How sad!

This reasoning depends, however, on Adam's being able to know what Eve would do at a stage of the game which will not be reached if the reasoning is valid. That sets a problem, since Eve's rational choices are premised on her knowledge that Adam is a rational agent and we appear just to have proved that a rational agent kills the game at the start. So, it seems, if he were to take only one coin, she must suspend the premise and choose her strategy in the light of the fact that he is not a rational agent. What now happens when she asks herself whether Adam, having let the game get so far, would let it continue again if she takes only one coin?

She has two possible lines of reasoning. One is that Adam is indeed not a rational agent, and either cannot reason straight or is not motivated to maximise his utility. But this leaves her stranded. If he is so incompetent that he cannot manage the simplest inferences, he might do anything whatever. If he is not a utility maximiser, the theory of rational strategic choice has no guidance to offer – a nasty blow to the pretensions of its whole approach.

Her other line is to look for method in Adam's madness. He may have reckoned that if her reading of his play leads her to cooperate, he will do better than he would by killing the game. But then he may be a rational agent after all. If so, what is his strategy? Well, it cannot be to cooperate to the very end, because no rational agent can settle for (3,3), when (4,2) is on offer and (4,2) takes account of *all* relevant consequences. But, if his strategy is to cooperate until stage n and then rat, hers is to cooperate only as far as stage $n-1$; and this thought restarts the backward induction. Hence she faces a paradox. If Adam is a rational agent playing out of equilibrium, then her rational strategy is not to cooperate, thus proving him not to be a rational agent. If he is not one, however, it may be rational for her to cooperate, thus making it possible that he is indeed a rational agent, with whom she has just proved it irrational to cooperate.

The conclusion portended is not exactly that backward induction is an invalid form of argument but rather, given the emergence of a paradox, that it does not yield a determinate choice of strategy for rational agents with common knowledge of their rationality. This result looks so quirky that we cannot decently let it stand. With a million coins on the table, it would be a scandal if reason truly recommended killing the game at once, not least because in practice sane people, who know each other to be sane, would do nothing of the sort. Experiments with such games show that some players get to the end, thus sharing the full total, and that most get most of the way. If reason disapproves, so much the worse for reason!

What to do about it is a slippery question and I mean only to offer reasons why the snag cannot be dealt with by applying the formal apparatus of advanced game theory with greater rigour. What conclusion shall we draw? We might conclude that sane people anchor their reasoning externally to the apparatus of game theory, for instance in an inductive argument that someone who has taken one coin so far will do so next time. This credits them with a non-strategic way of deciding what to do and implies that the abstraction which populates the idealised world of fully rational choices omits something vital for choice in everyday life. Then what exactly? It could be, for instance, habit, construed as a non-rational tendency to behave in a regular way, in the spirit of Hume's contention that all our reasonings rest in the end on habit and custom. This, however, would be another blow to the hopes of reason.

Alternatively, it could be that sane people make implicit agreements when playing centipede games. Adam opens by taking only one coin, thus making Eve an offer, which she accepts by taking only one coin; and so on. This seems plausible enough, if we regard everyday folk as capable of making and keeping promises. It also looks more consistent with everyday ideas of rationality – or reasonableness – than does a final reference to habit. But the question is still what makes people capable of promising and, if the answer is to lie along the Enlightenment trail, we still need to answer it consistently with an Enlightened account of rationality and rational agents.

There are two plausible technical moves to make at this point. One is to inject considerations of probability. If Adam thinks there is a probability, however small, that Eve will play across, if he does, then he hesitates. If he then reflects that, given common knowledge of rationality, this hesitation will enter her calculations, he has further reason to hesitate. In other words, uncertainty, once injected, breeds uncertainty by multiplying it in mutual calculations infinitely embedded in one another. Hence an initially tiny probability of cooperation may be enough to make cooperation rational. In that case, the obvious fact that real people often cooperate does not prove them not to be game-theoretically rational agents.

In reply, I accept that there are elegant theorems about probabilities, which might do the trick once the way has been cleared for them. But I do not think that they can be simply conjured up. Standard ideas of probability are to do with what is likely to happen to a single agent in an independent environment. For instance, whether Robinson Crusoe is rational to make a net depends on the probability of extra fish; and the fish do not have plans which include Crusoe's. Here the environment, although not static, can serve as an independent basis for his calculations. When Friday appears, on the other hand, each has to allow for what the other is likely to do, with Crusoe's estimate depending on what he takes Friday's to be and *vice versa*. The regress involved suspends the standard theory of probability, while a notion of strategic probability is worked out. That raises the original question about strategic choice for ideally rational agents in a different but still unanswered form.

The other technical move sets off from the evident fact that people do not always behave in repeated games as they do in one-shot games. In real life, Hume's farmers will get on better this year if they expect to play the game again next year. So it would be a mistake to draw general conclusions from isolated encounters. Game theory too can distinguish between one-shot games and a series or supergame, thus clearing the way for intuitively more appealing conclusions about what it is rational to do in a game which will be repeated. Enjoyably, the riddle of backward induction crops up again if the game is to be repeated a definite number of times. Since it is irrational to play cooperatively in the final game of a series, players will therefore not cooperate in the last but one, the last but two. . .and so on back to the very first. But, for a series of infinite, indefinite or unknown length, technical demonstrations can be given that it is rational to play across in any particular game.

In reply, I again accept the technicalities. But there is still a question about what is going on. The obvious effect of embedding a game in a series is to introduce new sticks and carrots, because, for instance, penalties for defection can operate and it becomes profitable to acquire a good reputation. The obvious way to describe this difference is to say that (net) pay-offs change for each game in the series. But then we no longer have the problem originally set. Conversely, if the all-things-considered pay-offs in each game remain as stated originally, then the problem stands. Technically, it may be possible to keep the same pay-offs and change the outcome, if the players are thought of as playing the supergame as a complex one-shot game in place of the original one-shot game. But that still ignores or obscures the crux, which remains whether and how rational agents can override the dictates of utility numbers assigned by ordering preferences according to the agent's ranking of consequences. The difficulty is one about representing promises in a consequentialist language and I deny that a formal theory has resources for the purpose which philosophers lack.

These replies both rely on the preceding ambiguity in the notion of utility. It cannot be a wholly procedural notion, innocent of all psychology. Its accompanying psychology connects rationality to motivation, even if there is a puzzle about whether pleasure and pain can be tempered to do the job. Motivation is to do with satisfying an agent's own passions, desires or preferences, under the aegis of a philosophical egoism which rules out any other way of taking it. The Benthamite move is to ensure commensurability by insisting that all actions generate utility as a consequence and that rational action maximises the utility available. It opens the way for a felicific calculus, which rational choice and game theory can extend very elegantly. But, granted the continuing need for some psychology, if the upshot is to be an account of what makes action rational, it does not subvert the starting point. This may still seem cavalier treatment of the technical refinements at which game theorists excel. But, to repeat, I am not ruling out a formal exercise which shows that rational agents have a determinate strategy in the centipede other than killing it at the start, regardless of length. The point is that, if the strategy changes the game so that pay-offs change, the problem has merely been postponed; and, if it leaves the pay-offs untouched, it is inconsistent with the psychology considered so far.

'So far' leaves it open whether there is scope for a more complex psychology within a philosophy of action which is desire-driven and consequentialist. We shall see.

CONCLUSION: PRUDENCE IN PERIL

Meanwhile, prudence is in peril. This is plain, if we have only self-regarding motives which reason must serve to the limit. Here prudence can recommend only fear inspired by institutions, like legal penalties for breach of contract and social sanctions for ignoring norms. The idea is to encourage mutual confidence and security, thus promoting the benefits to be had from cooperation. This is its only way to help reconcile the interests of each with the interests of all. But instituting such arrangements is one thing and abiding by them another. Short of a horrendous system of policing, Adam and Eve retain an incentive to do better for themselves on occasions when evasion is worth the risk. Crucially, where an agent's interests diverge from the interests of all, fear is not fully effective in ensuring that each acts in the interests of all. Thus, the final player in the 'centipede' retains a reason for reneging and will act on it unless afraid of consequences which are only as sure as penalties and sanctions are effective. The other player will realise this and opt out sooner, thus starting a backward induction which defeats both their interests. But, although this is sad for both, there is nothing which either can do about it.

Yet this can hardly be the end of the road for prudence, and widening a rational agent's motives to include sympathy looks helpful. It certainly makes the crux less common. But it is striking to find Hume himself first introducing sympathy and then arguing that it is not enough. His reason goes deep. The perils of prudence arise from our natural partiality towards ourselves, in his view. All our natural passions and natural morality are shot through with a 'partiality' which favours those nearer to us in one way or another. Sympathy widens the boundary to include more people than purely self-regarding motives would favour. But, since it is 'partial', this widening does nothing to make us impartial between those we care about and those we do not. A civilised society is possible, he believes, only if we can be impartial, dealing even-handedly between those nearer and further from our affections, between those within our ken and strangers.

If he is right, prudence remains in peril. It would be prudent for Adam and Eve to make and keep an agreement to sup at The Triumph of Reason, since both will do better thereby than by getting stuck at the start. But, so far, the instrumental rationality which makes them prudent also makes them unable to trust one another. The obstacle is plain enough. It is that a rational Adam with a choice between four coins and three, or between his favourite pub and one he likes less overall, prefers more to less and better to worse. Since the underlying calculations are in utils, which take all sources of satisfaction into account, an injection of sympathy may affect some apparent examples of the problem but does not touch its core. This more technical chapter has only reinforced the previous one.

A further thought is that having reached the final node could be a reason for preferring the lesser utility of keeping to plan to the greater of taking advantage. This sounds consistent with prudence, not least because it allows the other player let the game reach the end. But, while prudential reasons are always forward-looking, we cannot suggest it. Bygones being always bygones, it is as if the present node and any still ahead were always a new game. This goes not only for the trust involved in the present game but, relatedly, for any apparent reinforcing of trust by thoughts of later games with the same player or, for that matter, with other players. By strengthening the weight of future consequences, we make defection less common. Yet we cannot remove it while reasons for being amiable remain only forward-looking.

Hence, for rational agents as construed so far, trust sets a problem not soluble within reason. But perils can sometimes be overcome and hopes of rescue are not exhausted.

4
A remedy in the judgement and understanding?

Hume's farmers are still about to lose both their harvests for want of mutual confidence and security. Although greater sympathy for one another might help, Hume is clear that sympathy is not enough. The problem set by our natural partiality is not solved by pointing out that we are often partial to our neighbours as well as to our friends. It is set by our natural inability to be impartial. To let us rise above this inconvenience of human nature and so overcome the perils of prudence, he therefore gives practical reason a twist.

He makes his move while discussing the origins of property and justice. Our natural sympathy and generosity are too limited to overcome the scanty provision which nature has made for our wants, he remarks, and too partial to ourselves to underpin the secure social framework needed if the benefits of cooperation are not to elude us. Hence all viable societies provide rules which secure ownership and an impersonal scheme of duties. These rules are artificial. In the *Enquiry* he notes the sheer variety of them in different societies and argues that, since the sentiments inherent in our universal human nature cannot account for it, the rules must be credited to reason and custom.[1] In the *Treatise* he contends that our natural ideas of morality, far from counteracting our natural partiality, serve to reinforce it. Hence justice, which enjoins impartiality, is an artificial virtue and the remedy which it offers is an artificial remedy:

> The remedy, then, is not derived from nature, but from *artifice*, or, more properly speaking, nature provides a remedy, in the judgement and understanding, for what is irregular and incommodious in the affections.[2]

We might still want to inject the remedy directly into the affections by postulating a natural instinct for justice or sense of duty as the root for the obligations which the remedy prescribes. Why are justice, honesty, gratitude and other motives with a temptingly normative character not among our original affections? The reason Hume gives in part II, section I is that mere regard to the virtue of an action cannot be the first motive of the action. Thus, although we have a duty to care for our children, we are moved to care for them in the first instance by natural affection, as distinct from duty. This is a tricky passage, since it seems to assume what it seeks to prove. The assumption is that philosophical egoism implies partiality even in our natural virtues; and one would like that demonstrated. But he is very insistent. Rules of property and justice intervene between the promptings of our affections and the actions to which they would otherwise lead. They arise from artifice, by way of conventions approved by the judgement and understanding. They are an artificial remedy for a natural partiality.

The remedy identifies what it takes to coax Adam and Eve past The Foole – the obstacle to a solution based on sanctions of all sorts. But trouble is looming at The Sensible Knave. This hostelry is named after the slippery customer who turns up in paragraph 232 of the *Enquiry*. The sensible knave 'may think that an act of iniquity or infidelity will make a considerable addition to his fortune, without causing any considerable breach in the social union and confederacy'. Despite the

1. *Enquiry Concerning the Principles of Morals*, III. II.
2. *Treatise*, book III, part II, section 2.

remedy, however, Hume finds it hard to muster a convincing retort. Can the knave not see that honesty is the best policy? Yes, but only up to this awkward point:

> That *honesty is the best policy*, may be a good general rule, but is liable to many exceptions; and he, it may perhaps be thought, conducts himself with most wisdom, who observes the general rule, and takes advantage of all the exceptions.

Always engagingly open-minded about his own philosophy, Hume admits himself stumped for an answer to the knave, 'if his heart rebel not against such pernicious maxims'. Yet the crux is not resolved by transferring it from head to heart, and, after a few more lines poking about to no avail, he signs off with the comment that such knaves are too smart for their own good. They are 'in the end, the greatest dupes, and have sacrificed the invaluable enjoyment of a character, with themselves at least, for the acquisition of worthless toys and gewgaws'.

This parting shot in fact offers a fresh line, with its suggestion that the sensible knave has forfeited the ability to live at peace with himself. But, although indeed worth pursuing, it is not a line readily open to Hume himself. Among his best-known themes are his treatment of the self as a bundle of perceptions and his relatedly negative concept of freedom as the power of acting, or not acting, according to the determination of the will. Given these presumptions, the question becomes an empirical one of whether sensible knaves do in fact cease to enjoy self-respect; and its answer is presumably that some do, some do not. To make more of it, a more robust self and a correspondingly positive notion of freedom would be needed. So I shall ignore this tempting avenue for the moment.

Meanwhile, the idea that nature provides a remedy in the judgement and understanding for what is irregular and incommodious in the affections is unconvincing in its Humean context. In a moral psychology where 'reason alone cannot be a motive to any action of the will', how can such a remedy bind us *in foro interno*? That is the original problem all over again. The artifice must fail, unless it can persuade sensible knaves, and hence rational individuals, to override their pay-offs by keeping their word even when they would do better not to. Other-regarding passions like sympathy and gratitude may often temper the pay-offs and so make the puzzle less common and urgent. But they do not help on occasions when the revised pay-offs still leave the final performer rationally bound not to perform, thus unravelling any promise to sup at The Triumph of Reason. Since Hume differs interestingly from Hobbes, he may perhaps have steered Adam and Eve past The Foole; but it looks as if the drinks are on him at The Sensible Knave.

A remedy in the judgement and understanding still looks attractive, however. Reason may be only the slave of the passions but its office includes pointing out the advantages of artifice. What could be more prudent than a system of justice and property which lets two farmers form a binding agreement and thus both get their harvests in? Yes, but the problem is not to spot the solution but to see how it could work. How can justice, as an artificial virtue, bind *in foro interno*? How can prudence forge the missing link between truth, virtue and happiness? To see exactly what is needed, here is a brisk reprise of the crux and then the shape of things to come.

PERILS OF STRATEGIC CHOICE

We are still working within a desire / belief model of action, where desire supplies the motor. Although the motivating desires need not be selfish, they must be the agent's own. In this precise sense, they still have to be 'self-interested'. Although they can take forms which vary with social context and culture, they activate a psychology which is universal. This psychology can be pretty schematic and procedural. But, while we retain the Enlightenment aim of grounding the social sciences in a primary science of mind, it must have some elements of substance. Minimally, it is a psychology where reason calculates the expected utility of the consequences of alternative actions for the satisfaction of the agent's own preferences. This just meets the case, provided that 'preference' and 'satisfaction' retain enough psychic reality to fill a threatened vacuum.

Prudence can certainly recommend enlightened self-interest. 'Think ahead', it advises, 'Play long', 'Sow now to reap later', 'Be of good repute.' This is shrewd, instrumental advice, favouring cooperation, whenever cooperation pays. But it is always addressed to a single agent, with the good of others relevant only in so far as furthering it benefits the agent, all things considered. This remains so even for an agent moved by natural sympathy, once pay-offs have been adjusted accordingly. Prudence may advise saints to be totally self-effacing, since their utility comes wholly from the utility of others. But saints are too rare to yield the solution needed, necessarily so when one reflects that a community of saints would set an intractable reflexive question of whose preferences are to motivate each saint. We have as yet no psychology where Adam can be impartial between himself and others, or where Eve can prefer the good of a partnership, when it differs from her own ranking of the outcomes.

This all creates a quandary for prudence when it comes to crucial occasions of strategic choice. It would indeed be prudent for farmer Adam to help farmer Eve with her harvest tomorrow if that were the only way to secure her help today. But, in practice at least, it often is not. Then prudence has a serpent's office in squeezing the maximum benefit from his marginal cost–benefit calculation. Does Adam take any intrinsic pleasure in helping Eve? Not beyond any already in the overall calculation. Does her help depend on whether he will in fact help her or on whether she believes that he will? The latter. Are there latent costs of defaulting which would outweigh the benefits? No. Very well, prudence advises agreeing to help tomorrow, without intending to do so. It advises the wholly selfish never to give a sucker an even break. Less obviously but no less firmly, it also advises the averagely unselfish to do likewise after allowing for any sympathy for suckers.

Since prudence is also telling Eve not to believe a word Adam says, it seems a pleasingly self-defeating guide to social collaboration. Yet there may be a distinction between the ideal-type case and the everyday one rehearsed in the last paragraph. Ideally, Adam is so transparent to Eve that he cannot deceive her into believing that he means to cooperate when prudence is telling him not to. So it may be that he can secure her help today only if he genuinely intends to help her in return tomorrow, thus changing what prudence advises. This thought, if right, sets some problems about the relation between the ideal and everyday cases, which we shall come to. But it also sets problems of its own about how today's intention to help tomorrow can persist tomorrow, when the help will have been received and there will be advantage in not reciprocating. I shall argue next that the difficulty goes deep, because, for the desire/belief model as so far presented, the agent lacks the steadfastness required and, in any case, joint action is always secondary.

To take the last point first, the collective outcome, when Adam and Eve do something together, is a sum of their individual choices, each of which is to be accounted for separately and in instrumental terms. Adam's contribution is Adam's individually rational choice; Eve's is Eve's. Although each of them figures in the other's calculations, they are like two methodological solipsists or windowless monads, each with an individual point of view containing the other's within it. There is no corporate body whose members they are. When Adam is trying to thread a needle, success does not depend on separate strategic choices by his right and left hands, each deciding where best to position itself, after considering what the other will do, since all choices are Adam's. But this offers no analogy for harvesting as a corporate action, since Adam and Eve are not a corporation and, at this stage of the argument, any cooperation can only be an outcome of individuals each choosing separately and strategically.

This monocular view of joint action has some disconcerting implications. Indeed, it implies that even simple coordination requires a remedy in the judgement and understanding for what is incommodious in the affections, as I shall argue in chapter 7. Less surprisingly, it blocks an obvious way forward, when the problem is that mutual compliance, although second best for all, is not what everyone *most* wants. Thus a convention which would suit everyone better than mutual defection in 'The Prisoner's Dilemma' (diagram below) sets a problem, because defection is everyone's dominant choice. Prudence here points out to Adam that, if Eve chooses X, he does better to choose Y (since 4 beats 3), and that, if she chooses Y, he also does better to choose Y (since 2 beats 1); and hence that he does better to choose Y, *whatever she chooses*. It gives Eve similar advice. Yet the resulting YY is worse for both than XX. This notorious logic of dominance undermines many norms and agreements, to the disadvantage of all, including free-riders. It is a constant element in the various troubles besetting Hobbes' treatment of covenants involving delayed performance, Hume's sad farmers and an Enlightenment Trail, where the lure of The Extra Trick should therefore make all progress past The Rational Choice unachievable by rational agents.

Eve

		X	Y
	X	3, 3	1, 4
Adam			
	Y	4, 1	2, 2

The Prisoner's Dilemma

Real-life examples abound. For instance, an ecological disaster is presently hitting some states of America because farmers are grazing so many cattle on the common land that the grass cannot regrow. No one intends or wants this result; but each helps to produce it, because each, choosing strategically whether to graze more animals, finds it rational to do so, whatever others choose. The sum of their choices is what has become known as a 'tragedy of the commons'. The fact that free-riders end up among the losers makes Hume's suggestion of a remedy in the judgement and understanding all the more appealing. But rational agents in the grip of a dominant strategic choice are rationally bound to reject the remedy in practice, whatever they may say about its merits in theory. Prudence makes sensible knaves of us all.

Sensible knaves are not to be trusted when trust depends on a normative expectation that they will act contrary to the dictates of their overall utility, as when keeping a promise which prudence deems better broken. There is no such snag for problems of coordination. Since any way of coordinating is a best solution for each and all, sensible knaves can be expected to stick to whatever convention emerges. A convention like 'Keep left' on the highway is underwritten by a safe prediction that rational agents will abide by it, because they have no reason not to. Hence some 'cooperative games' (those where any agreement can be counted on) can be analysed in terms of 'non-cooperative games' (those where agreements are kept by each player because doing so is an individually maximising strategy). But an expectation of compliance which relies on predictions got by noting that compliance maximises utility for each player is not the kind of expectation which yields a solution to games where cooperation is not any individual's maximising strategy. The problem of trust calls for normative expectations which can cement agreements despite calculations of marginal utility.

Here one asks again whether rational choice and game theory can escape the elenchus by technical finesse, especially when the game is reiterated. But what was said in the last chapter about long centipedes and repeated play still stands. The root of the perversity goes too deep. Having distinguished predictive from normative expectations, we find that we cannot make sense of the latter under the aegis of instrumentally rational choice. They give no independent leverage and so cannot account for the undoubted fact that people do cooperate on occasions when their individual expected utility calculations are against it. The difficulty remains that promises and agreements, when represented in consequential terms, lose their power to bind a rational agent. Technicalities and factors introduced by repeating the game may reduce the number of occasions when words need to be more than cheap talk. But they do not eliminate them and, crucially, the problem of trust cannot be made to vanish in this way.

Humean moral psychology cannot distinguish predictive from normative expectations within a realm of strategic choice, because motivation is always a matter of the agent's own preferences. The addition of fellow-feeling may ease Adam and Eve past The Foole by making their affections less incommodious, because less wholly self-regarding; but, because it does nothing to weaken the philosophical egoism, they cannot escape The Sensible Knave. Hume sees the problem but can take us no further along the trail himself.

IMPARTIALITY AND FAIRNESS

This is a good moment to recall that Adam and Eve have not really even started. We let them reach the middle of the trail very much for the sake of argument. But it is clear by now that prudence cannot recommend their subscribing to a version of a social contract which leaves their philosophical egoism undisturbed. Although the contract offers better consequences for each subscriber, the offer is idle unless everyone who subscribes will also keep the agreement on occasions when their own pay-off for breaking it is better still. Any successful contract involves adopting a standpoint which is impartial between subscribers when each comes to decide what to do. Hume's remedy in the judgement and understanding is to detach us from the partiality accompanying the natural virtues; and we can agree that success would improve the prospect of supper at The Triumph of Reason. But the question is how Adam and Eve can act on what they see to be impartially better for both, given the lure of what is better still for each. An impartial standpoint may be the answer but not while they are motivated as philosophical egoism supposes.

Although Hume floats the idea, the attempt to harness reason to impartiality is more often associated with Adam Smith. In *The Theory of Moral Sentiments*, he credits us with some natural sympathies but not enough to stretch far. If an earthquake swallowed up the great empire of China with all its myriads of inhabitants, he remarks, a man of humanity in Europe would no doubt express sorrow and reflect on the precariousness of human life.

> And when all this fine philosophy was over, when all these humane sentiments had been fairly expressed, he would pursue his business or his pleasure, take his repose or his diversion, with the same ease and tranquillity, as if no such accident had happened. The most frivolous disaster which could befall himself would occasion a more real disturbance. If he was to lose his little finger tomorrow, he would not sleep tonight. But, provided he never saw them, he

will snore with the most profound security over the ruin of a hundred million of his brethren, and the destruction of that immense multitude seems plainly an object less interesting to him, than this paltry misfortune of his own.[3]

To offset this limitation, however, he assigns us 'an impartial spectator in our breasts', whose office is to identify even-handed solutions to conflicts arising through bias to ourselves. The capacity to be impartial is (*pace* Hume) among our natural endowments. So, if an impartial spectator would think The Triumph of Reason the pub which offers most all round, then a rational Adam would accept this judgement and a rational Eve would give him the chance to act on it.

The metaphor of a spectator in our breasts can be read in different ways. We might regard this impartial fellow as a resident Inspector General, who is ready to arbitrate between ourselves and others. But that suggests an intervention after the event, when Adam has grabbed more than his share and needs to be told to hand some back, for instance as he drowns his conscience in the bar of The Extra Trick. In that case, however, I do not see that an impartial spectator could do more than buy the drinks with an admiring shrug of the shoulders. The job which needs doing occurs further back down the trail, when Adam is contemplating a strategy which involves breaking an agreement. The spectator's task is not merely to point out that the strategy will fail, because Eve is too much of a rational agent to let him get away with it. It is to show him that it would be an inferior strategy, even if it were to succeed.

That seems a tall order, since it involves convincing Adam that it is sometimes better not to choose an action which has greater expected utility for himself. How can a rational agent come to believe this? The spectator proceeds in two steps, I fancy, first by giving an impartial reading of the situation and then by trying to persuade Adam to be guided accordingly. The impartial reading is a matter of comparing outcomes which distribute various utility totals between two

---

3. *The Theory of Moral Sentiments* (1759), ed. D. Raphael and A. Macfie, Oxford: Clarendon Press, 1976, pp. 136–7.

unidentified agents, as in the next diagram. Then, by way of persuasion, the spectator can invoke the Pareto principle from welfare economics. Uncontentiously, outcome (a) can be rejected, because there is another where *both* agents do better. Scarcely more contentiously, outcome (b) can be rejected because there is another where at least one agent does better and no one does worse. Having pointed this out, the spectator bows politely, smiles impartially and awaits Adam's reaction.

Outcome	Total	Distribution	
(a)	2	0 + 2	(The Rational Choice)
(b)	8	5 + 3	(The Extra Trick)
(c)	9	5 + 4	(The Triumph of Reason)

An impartial spectator's reading

Adam cannot deny that, if the problem is indeed whether $(5 + 4)$ is superior to $(5 + 3)$, with all relevant information included and all irrelevant information excluded, $(5 + 4)$ is superior. That is, for instance, what he would have to say if set the problem in the abstract, perhaps on a training course for impartial spectators. It is what he would have said, let us suppose, if he were smitten with temporary amnesia and no longer knew how exactly the specified utils were to be allotted between Eve and himself. So we might hope that, even when knowing himself to be the agent who gets the '5' in (b) and the '4' in (c), it is still what he will say, thereby accepting a sufficient reason to act accordingly.

But philosophical egoism is still in play and, given Adam's affections, this last bit of information looks awkwardly relevant and distinctly incommodious. On the other hand, willingness to act on it has a large price. If that is what a rational agent would do, Eve would know it and not give him the chance. So, reason can suggest, the fact that he would do better to settle for The Triumph of Reason than not to advance beyond the very first pub makes it rational for him to forgo The Extra Trick, when he gets there. For Eve would let him have that final choice if and only if it is what a rational agent would conclude, when the moment of choice arrives.[4]

This very nearly does the trick, in my view. It offers to temper the bargain-hunting character of ideally rational agents just enough, so that they no longer lose an excellent bargain because they cannot resist a marginally better one. It would stop rational action being ultimately self-defeating, and do so without subverting the rational choice basis of the desire/belief model. But, when we take it slowly, three large obstacles appear.

Firstly, in what exact spirit would Adam now pass The Rational Choice? It is not merely because doing so is required for the impartially best outcome, since, so far, reason alone can never be a motive to any action of the will. It has to be because Adam himself expects to do better thereby. This in turn requires that he intends at this early stage to pass The Extra Trick too. Yet he knows, and so does Eve, that a rational agent, faced with a choice between 5 utils and 4 utils, chooses 5. He knows it because a rational agent's reasons for action are still always forward-looking, with the utility numbers scored after taking all relevant consequences into account. This creates a major problem about the intention to keep on going, which is to be formed at the start of the trail. It seems that this initial intention either is worthless, because it is sure to be overturned later, or, since Adam recognises this, cannot even be formed.

Can Adam overcome this snag by making a suitably public agreement with Eve? No, not unless the agreement is binding *in foro interno*. But its being public does not make it so, unless publicity creates a sanction which changes the net utilities and hence his ranking of the pubs. Otherwise it is either reliable only until put to the test or, as with an 'intention' one expects to cancel later, cannot be genuine. The point is nicely caught in a couplet deriding David Lloyd George, the distrusted British Prime Minister after the 1914–18 war:

---

4. For a skilful defence of this line, see David Gauthier, 'Commitment and choice: an essay on the rationality of plans', in S. Farina, F. Hahn and S. Vannucci (eds)., *Ethics, Rationality and Economic Behaviour*, Oxford: Clarendon Press, 1996. pp. 217–43.

Call not his broken promises a crime:
he meant them – how he meant them – at the time.

So how does Adam bind himself *in foro interno*? The incentive is great – supper at The Triumph of Reason instead of The Rational Choice or, less figuratively, his second best outcome instead of his second worst. It is worth trying for a model of rational choice with room for an agent able to make and carry out a plan to this effect. Suppose, for example, we credit Adam with a suitable disposition, like steadfastness of character, which will take him past The Extra Trick as a price worth paying to advance along the trail at all. That is no simple proposal, however.[5] Since it involves intending now to override what he correctly foresees will be his preferences at a later stage, it requires a major revision of the model. But, since the Enlightenment project is faltering, unless it is rational to keep agreements in defiance of utilities, let us not be daunted.

The immediate question is how we are to conceive of Adam over time. Although I have been speaking as if he were unpuzzlingly the same enduring person throughout, this is misleading. The motor all along has been his desires or preferences at the moment of action, and the continuity of the self has consisted, in effect, in their overall continuity or coherence over time. To make the proposal work, however, we must embrace a crucial discontinuity. If Adam were parachuted onto the trail at the final node, he would choose The Extra Trick. How can it matter that he has in fact arrived there by walking along the trail, armed with a plan to go further? Can the model be squared with the suggestion that, sometimes, bygones are *not* bygones? So far, it is as if Adam were a series of bundles of preferences, connected by close resemblance between neighbouring bundles but with no enduring and substantive self, whose preferences they are. It is as if the Adam making the final choice were not the author of the plan but the author's great-great-grandson, call him Adam II.

5. Witness Edward McLennen's pioneering theory of resolute choice in his *Rationality and Dynamic Choice*, Cambridge University Press, 1990, which is much in Gauthier's mind in the article just cited.

This Adam II can reasonably ask why he is bound by his ancestor's commitments. In the absence of a metaphysical person or enduring identical self, we can try to answer by taking the analogy with successive generations very seriously. In some societies ancestors' commitments can impose normative expectations on their children's children. But we cannot simply inject this thought into a rational choice story. If we want to invest a theory of instrumental choice with an apparatus of norms involving notions like lineage, gratitude or honour in socially situated selves, we shall need many preliminaries, not least a suitable solution to the problem of trust itself. Otherwise, any child of the Enlightenment must object that the plans of the dead cannot bind the living. In any case, an appeal to normative expectations is the wrong sort of move as a part of an attempt to show that a truly rational agent will *predictably* ignore the temptation of The Extra Trick. The right sort of move is to complicate the agent, so that reason has more to work on than the preferences which its only office so far is to serve and obey.

That brings us to the second obstacle. However quite we conceive of the self, the relations among reason, preference and action need rethinking. This emerged when we failed to see how Hume's remedy could overcome incommodious affections by subjecting them to reason-guided judgement, or how Smith's impartial spectator could introduce self-distancing into the model. We cannot simply inject a will, with the power to countermand the results of deliberation conducted in the service of the passions, into a model where reason alone can never be a motive to any action of the will. A more complex, perhaps two-tier, self is needed. I am all for this in general, and there are current discussions to draw on, starting from Harry Frankfurt's distinction between first-order and second-order preferences.[6] Not everyone is happy with their preferences. There are, for instance, alcoholics who would rather not be alcoholics: they prefer whisky to

6. H. G. Frankfurt, 'Freedom of the will and the concept of a person', *Journal of Philosophy*, 68 (1971), reprinted in his *The Importance of What We Care About*, Cambridge University Press, 1988.

water but also prefer that they prefer (or come to prefer) water to whisky. Such conflicts are common enough to suggest adopting a richer moral psychology, where agents have preferences over their preferences and where reason, when called to take sides, endorses the higher tier. Then Adam may be able to override his immediate, first-order preference for The Extra Trick by appeal to a preference for being someone who prefers to complete his plans and keep his agreements.

Yes, but it is not obvious that reason always favours the higher order. For example a guilt-ridden homosexual, who prefers his own sex, while also preferring to prefer the other, might well do better to set about shedding his feelings of guilt rather than suppress his sexual orientation. So what exactly is reason being asked to do? Is its task to decide which preference is easier to live with (or harder to eradicate) or is the question to do with the agent's real and true preferences or, on a different note, with the right regulative ideal to guide one's life? Amid these uncertainties, it is plain at least that a more complex self calls for deep reflection, not a casual fiat which resolves Adam's immediate quandary without heed for further implications.[7]

The third obstacle is to explain how a judgement based on higher-order preferences can translate into action. Reason is by now being given an office which does more than serve and obey Adam's preferences in a humble, if ingenious, way. For, if Adam's current preferences at any moment made him more of a gentleman than a dastard, the remedy recommended by Hume and Smith would not be needed. By now, reason is being asked to umpire between desires of different

---

7. That higher-order preferences are not always trumps was well argued by Gary Watson in 'Free agency', *Journal of Philosophy*, 72 (1975), pp. 205–20. Frankfurt himself has since refined his concept of a person, notably in the title essay in *The Importance of What We Care About*, and, in the same volume, 'Identification and wholeheartedness'. See also 'On the usefulness of final ends', *Iyyun: The Jerusalem Philosophical Quarterly*, 41 (1992), pp. 3–19; 'On the necessity of ideals', in G. C. Noam and T. Wesen, eds., *The Moral Self*, Cambridge, Mass.: MIT Press, 1993; and 'Autonomy, necessity and love', in H. Fulda and R.-P. Horstmann (eds.), *Vernunftbegriffe in der Moderne*, Stuttgart: Klett-Cotta, 1994. The refinements, however, take him too far from a rational-choice account to pursue here.

orders, or indeed, we may be starting to suspect, between desires and something else, for instance ideals.

Here lies a formidable issue in the philosophy of mind, which I can only indicate here. We have not yet rejected Hume's dictum that 'reason alone can never be motive to any action of the will', and many philosophers insist that he is right about that. Bernard Williams, for instance, has always maintained that every action requires an 'internal reason', something already in the agent's 'subjective motivational set' to supply a given desire for reason to serve.[8] Other philosophers, often taking a lead from Kant, whom I shall summon up in the next chapter, are equally adamant that 'external reasons' are possible, since agents can sometimes be moved to act contrary to their preferences, inclinations or desires. Thomas Nagel, for example, holds that altruism is possible for an agent who must first overcome a disinclination and that there is a 'view from nowhere' which can (just) be adopted by someone high-minded enough.[9] Although the dispute is complicated by the need to nuance notions of what can count as a desire and how or whether beliefs differ from desires, there is no mistaking the depth of disagreement. I mention it not to take sides but to indicate how radically an Adam, who can plan to override his later preferences and succeed, differs from the rational agents with whom we began.[10] There is no quick kill to be had from suggesting that Adam can be rea-

---

8. Especially in 'Internal and external reasons' in *Moral Luck*, Cambridge University Press, 1981, and related arguments in *Ethics and the Limits of Philosophy*, London: Fontana Books, 1985. An already broad notion of what can count as internal reason is broadened further in 'Values, reasons and the theory of persuasion' in S. Farina, F. Hahn and S. Vannucci (eds.), *Ethics, Rationality and Economic Behaviour*, Oxford: Clarendon Press, 1996, pp. 66–74.

9. See *The Possibility of Altruism*, Oxford University Press, 1970; and *The View from Nowhere*, Oxford University Press, 1986.

10. My own view is that external reasons are not only possible but also necessary and can motivate by being recognised as reasons. See 'External and internal reasons', chapter 6 of *The Cunning of Reason*, Cambridge University Press, 1988, and 'The shape of a life', in J. E. J. Altham and R. Harrison (eds.), *World, Mind and Ethics*, Cambridge University Press, 1995. The latter volume includes John McDowell's essay, 'Might there be external reasons?' and Williams' reply to it (pp. 186–94) and to mine (pp. 210–16).

soned into passing up The Extra Trick, and a final chance to maximise his utility, by reflecting that he does better to end at The Triumph of Reason than to opt out at the start.

Meanwhile, prudence is only in serious trouble over strategic choice. For a parametric choice by a single rational agent, prudence advises the maximising of utility overall; and, apart from a hint that the carrying out of plans may require a self with a standpoint outside the developing series of immediate preferences, I have not tried to be awkward about that. But strategic choice is thoroughly troublesome, since the keeping of agreements and promises cannot withstand a dominant reason to break them, while reason remains the slave of the passions. Adam can expect Eve to fall in with a plan which suits both of them only if she expects him to forgo a greater utility for himself. Tantalisingly, the upshot is an outcome which is inferior for both of them; and a remedy is easy to spot. If they could adopt an impartial spectator's advice, both would do better. But they can cooperate neither for the benefit of each, while that requires one of them to make an inferior final choice and the other to expect it, nor in their joint interest, while they have none.

Conclusion

The conclusion is not flatly that prudence is the wrong guide to trust, since there may still be scope for ingenuity. The gap to be bridged is there because the standard theory of rational choice defines rationality by reference to the agent's own expected utility, whereas trust requires that we can expect people to ignore this siren call. To bridge it, we can try noting that sympathy or fellow-feeling reduces the gap and that, even for a strictly self-interested agent, there are reasons to cooperate whenever reputation will matter in the future. But such thoughts can show only that the problem is critical less often than it looks. They do not begin to suggest that a rational agent can be trusted not to exploit trust when it would pay to do so. This remains the point which ingenuity must address.

In game-theoretic terms, trust requires out-of-equilibrium play – strategic choice which is not a best answer to the other player's move.

Although some game theorists are willing to entertain the idea, I believe that it needs a radical change in the agent before it can offer a fresh way to trust. The snag remains that utilities are states in the agent caused by events in the world, and expected utilities an estimate of how satisfying and how likely. This forward-looking scheme ensures that rational agents have a clear course when choosing at the final node of a centipede like the Enlightenment Trail. If, all things considered, The Extra Trick outranks The Triumph of Reason for Adam, then he is bound to reject The Triumph of Reason. The scheme requires that all reasons be translated into satisfactions and, thus homogenised, treated instrumentally. The fact that one choice involves keeping an agreement and the other involves breaking it can affect his assignment of utilities, but not what he does about them, once assigned.

This remains a shoddy rendering of what we fancy to be our motivation when we have moral reason to keep an incommodious promise. Prudence cannot agree; but it can be tempted by the thought that an impartial view pays better than a partial one. Yet this requires an agent who refuses to homogenise motivating elements which the scheme insists on homogenising. The very idea in turn requires a fresh kind of agent and a fresh notion of rationality. This agent is no less idealised than the old, but differently. The new Adam and Eve retain limits to their mutual knowledge, due to their being separate persons and so incompletely transparent. They have limits to their instrumental rationality because they can rise above their own point of view – a contentious claim which must wait for the next chapter. By now, however, the initial hope that agents can be treated as bundles of preferences, information and computing power is fading and the concept of instrumental rationality fast losing dominance. I am not saying flatly that prudence is exhausted; but I doubt if we can advance further by thinking in game-theoretic terms. The theory of games makes it elegantly clear why the old agents could not be trusted and offers no remedy within its standard approach.

To put the conclusion boldly, practical reasoning which can govern incommodious preferences in an agent capable of promising is not, *au fond*, instrumental and the agent is a person, as distinct from an ordered set of preferences. So is what an impartial spectator offers a *moral* point of view? There is still much to be said for trying to solve the problem of trust without adopting one. Since trust is common enough among people who disagree fundamentally in moral matters, it would be much tidier to avoid moral philosophy in explaining when and why it is rational to be both trusting and trustworthy. Yet impartiality soon shades into fairness which soon shades into morality. We must think about these connections, before pursuing the question of what it is to be rational.

5
Fairness and morality

Impartiality looks likely to help Adam and Eve on their way, since it detaches each from their own point of view. Yet it cannot simply be the detachment which gets Adam to think of all his states or selves, rather than those of the immediate moment, since his need to arbitrate between his earlier and later ones is unpuzzlingly for his own benefit. How he chooses among his present, earlier and later selves and whether he is to be identified with one, all or none of them are interesting questions. But, while nothing normative intrudes on the predictions of his present self about the actions of a later one, there is still a difference between two Adams and the relation of Adam to Eve.[1] With Adam and Eve to think about and trust at issue, impartiality turns trickier. Although they have become more complex since the start, being by now two-tier agents able to reflect that their preferences are interfering with their interests, they need something more before they can rule against themselves and trust one another.

Yet we seem to have dealt them some useful cards, if only they could play them. What is stopping them? Part of the answer, I think, is

---

1. For a fuller comparison of intrapersonal strategic choice with the interpersonal sort see *The Cunning of Reason*, chapter 6, on 'External and internal reasons'.

that for Adam alone there is finally only one point of view, whereas for Adam and Eve there are three: his, hers and theirs. Given the strong assumption of individualism, however, 'theirs' is an amalgam of his and hers, and impartiality is, in effect, anonymity between individuals – a device for disregarding who in particular gets what in a distribution of utilities. Prudence cannot simply advise individual Adam and individual Eve, separately or in alliance, to make an impartial point of view primary. (The point will be reinforced when we discuss coordination in chapter 7.) So there are two possible next moves, I fancy, neither straightforwardly open to prudence. One is to embed individuals in social relations so deeply that they become social first and individual only in some contexts, typically those of a modern market society. This will be tried in the next chapter. The other, to be tried now, is to treat the impartial spectator as the voice of an explicitly moral point of view.

Here prudence is tempted. On the one hand, most (but not all) moral philosophies hold that to act morally is to do what would be universally right or good, whatever the consequences for oneself; and prudence cannot simply endorse that. On the other hand, one may do better for oneself by acting morally. Then Adam and Eve, keeping their agreement for the reason that it is right or good to do so, will each be rewarded here on earth. Prudence finds this a very interesting thought, and one to be explored when we have said more about impartiality and fairness as possible links between enlightened self-interest and morality.

Impartiality looks a neutral idea and fairness most of the way to a moral one. An impartial spectator can recommend a distribution which favours the rich against the poor, provided that it does not favour named persons because of who they are. It treats equals equally and that is also part of the brief of fairness. But it can still be unfair that A is rich while B is poor. A market, dealing impartially between them, may treat B unfairly, because B cannot wait as long as A. Fairness is thus, like impartiality, a procedural notion but one with a moral tone, whereas merely impartial procedures may accept unfair situations. Yet this distinction depends on a prior one between what is procedurally right and substantively good. That would be untenable if what is procedurally right derives from what is good. This matters, because current versions of liberalism usually rely on being able to demonstrate what is right entirely without help from ideas of the good society or good life. We shall want to consider whether this is on.

Condorcet was clear that 'truth, virtue and happiness are bound together by an unbreakable chain'. That is the old fighting liberalism, which campaigns for liberal values as a matter of science. Kant is more ambiguous and there is a strong case for thinking that he defends only procedural liberal values, moral and political. This would let him defend his view of the character of morality and the form of a just society without, however, telling us anything of the content of the good life. Whether that represents him correctly is not crucial for the book but whether it can be done is. So, even if we find that fairness raises moral questions which impartiality avoids, we shall need to be careful about morality and fairness.

Meanwhile, Kant definitely offers a fresh way to construe morality by disconnecting moral reasons from desires and making them basic to rationality. That changes our strategy, if he is right, by subordinating instrumental rationality to a higher kind. The next part of the chapter will work this out and ask what a moral theory can rely on, if not the external morality of the universe. The second part will try some contractarian answers and the third will see whether, for Enlightenment purposes, trust depends on a Kantian line. The next chapter will contrast it with conditional moralities for culturally located agents, an attractive approach which the Enlightenment will resist. That will set the stage for the final reckoning.

PLAYING FAIR WITH KANT

There is something natural-seeming about a sense of fair play. Children are quick to exclaim 'That's not fair!' when another child gets more. Denied their wants by tyrannous parents, they are quick to appeal by laying comparative evidence of unequal treatment. The parents, thus arraigned for being unfair, must either concede or reject the comparisons because apparently similar cases are not similar. 'Yes, it is fair that you get more today, because you had less yesterday', they can retort, or 'No, you cannot have more cake just because you are older, bigger or greedier.' Such family exchanges suggest a spirit of fairness among the moral sentiments, which can be invoked and schooled so as to neutralise bias to oneself.

Yet this does nothing to settle whether a spirit of fair play is natural or, as Hume would say, artificial. Nor does it hint whether the demands of fair play are eternal, universal, natural, constructed or imposed to suit the interests of those, like parents, with the power to make them stick. Fairness has emerged as an uneasy blend of natural and artificial, in need of a third element. The former indicates a natural passion of a cool sort, akin to sympathy, although cooler, and surfacing only in moments of tranquillity. But, if it is simply a passion in competition with currently stronger passions, why does it ever win? Suppose that, on the one hand, Eve wants the last chocolate biscuit, and that, on the other hand, since she has had one already and Adam has not, she wants to leave it for him. If this is a tug-of-war whose outcome depends on the relative strength of these wants, how can fairness pull hard enough to win? The artificial element indicates not a passion of any temperature but an umpire's power of detachment from our passions, which lets us see ourselves as one person among others. Yet what gives this point of view its effectiveness and, relatedly, its authority? The question invites the conclusion that fairness does indeed involve taking a *moral* point of view. Whereas the idea of an impartial point of view could be introduced as a device for securing mutual self-interest, the idea of fair play shades rapidly into notions of virtue and moral obligation.

'Moral' is a slippery term. It is often used in a sociological vein to refer to *mores*, the sanctified customs which take different forms in different societies and are presumably functional in keeping the social wheels turning. If we construe it in this way, we shall be asking an observer's question about how societies function and the role of morally charged language in sanctioning breaches of the norms which secure trust. The observer's answer may well be that it is rational to be moral; but, if so, strictly in the sense that societies function best (or at all) only when their members internalise socially useful *mores*. This is not the spirit of our original question, however. In asking when and why is it rational for people to trust one another, we have not been putting silent quotation marks round 'rational' and 'moral'. We have been enquiring throughout on behalf of rational agents, whom morality, if rationally binding, binds *in foro interno*. The original question was addressed not to observers but to agents. Although agents need to know what other agents take to be right or good, they also ask, on their own account, what sort of considerations count as good reasons for action. The latter question is more fundamental; and it calls for a philosophical answer.

The last paragraph suggests a neat distinction between spectators and agents, with philosophers backing the former, provided that they deal in morality rather than *mores*. This may sound like begging the question against a naturalistic ethics which sets off from a human nature endowed with moral sentiments and derives moral conclusions from the facts of our 'moral psychology'. For instance, the Aristotelian tradition works with agents' actual virtues, construed objectively, and generates a spectator's standpoint from this moral phenomenology. I am not trying to rule it out. But there is a problem about the place and character of reason in such accounts; and I am taking my cue from Hume's advice that remedies in the judgement and understanding work against the grain of our natural sentiments. If so, reason upholds a universalism, which construes morality as a matter of acting on principle, and takes moral reasons to be those which apply to anyone or everyone so placed.

In an Enlightenment setting, the trail leads next to Immanuel Kant and the idea of a unique moral point of view enshrined in his moral philosophy. What Kantian progress to The Triumph of Reason demands is a Good Will. When Adam is tempted to take advantage of Eve, he is to ask himself whether his contemplated choice is in accordance with a 'maxim' applicable to everyone so placed. Unless he can will that everyone should rat on an agreement when it suits, he cannot be warranted in doing so himself. This is the condition of acting from a Good Will and of the autonomy which is the mark of a moral agent.

Since, by parity of reasoning, one cannot claim autonomy for oneself without recognising that others have the same claim, it follows that one should always treat other people as ends in themselves, never as means to one's own ends.

A disciple of Kant's moral philosophy is thus truly capable of promising. Adam cannot will that he may break his promises, unless he can will that everyone so placed may do likewise; and he cannot will this, because there would then be no promising. The imperative which attends the keeping of promises is, in Kant's terms, categorical. It does not say, 'Keep your promises if . . .', as a hypothetical imperative would. It does not say, 'Keep them if your desires are better served thereby; but break them if it suits you.' It does not say even, 'Keep them if the consequences of doing so are better for humanity at large.' The command of duty is categorical: 'Keep them!' There may be some sub-clauses to settle priorities when duties conflict. But there are no sub-clauses which let desires or consequences override the call of duty. A morally autonomous agent does what is right and damn the consequences.

A Kantian account of obligation, if adopted, makes light of the Enlightenment trail. Adam and Eve exchange promises and then act simply for the reason that they have promised. But there is much to think about before we can rest content. Kant offers a bold but disputable answer to the objection that there is nothing compelling enough about the moral point of view to lock rational agents onto it. His answer is not that it pays to be moral. For, although it does indeed pay, at least in the present case, this is a by-product in a theory where duty must be done whether it pays or not. His answer is that moral reasons for action are trumps for a rational agent and that they motivate rational agents simply by being recognised as relevant. This abrupt break with accounts of practical reason grounded in prudence and mutual self-interest invites several objections.

The most general is, I presume, that, even with Kant to guide us, we cannot leap the fact / value distinction so lightly or, indeed, at all. Condorcet, like many other Enlightenment thinkers, assumed that the human and social world would yield its secrets, when the methods of the scientific revolution were applied to it, as plentifully as nature at large. Among its secrets were truths of ethics, meaning truths about our moral psychology and hence both about how we should live and about the success or failure of particular *mores* in achieving a balance of interests and a sum of happiness. This vision, intoxicating to the enlightened, is horrible to romantics and post-moderns. Critics have persistently denounced its implications, starting with its rationale for the Terror and continuing with all totalitarian attempts to organise the good life scientifically, thus spreading death, misery and the destruction of the human spirit. In more abstract spirit, it offends against 'Hume's law', as analytical philosophy will put it. Hume denied that moral conclusions can be derived from factual premises, arguing that statements containing 'ought' introduced a relation which could be given no empirical or, without begging the question, *a priori* justification. That something is so never implies that anything should be so or should be done, except with the aid of further premises which then raise the same difficulty again. 'Hume's law' gives a powerful reason to respect the fact / value distinction.

Kant, however, is not Condorcet. He does not accept that nature has endowed us with sentiments which mean that, given suitable institutions and a spot of social engineering, truth, virtue and happiness can be run in harmony. Kantian autonomy is deeply different from Condorcet's idea of freedom as desire satisfied, as we shall see in chapter 8. Yet Kantian moral reasons for action are objective reasons, since it is an objective truth that a rational agent should act on universalisable maxims. In upshot, we are offered an account of rational action, and hence practical reason, which introduces a fresh notion of rationality with a moral charge, thus challenging the primacy of the instrumental notion relied on so far. Whether to accept the offer is critical.

The stakes are very high. A major reason for denying that statements of fact can serve as proof or evidence for statements of value derives from the scientific revolution itself. Previous understanding of the world had relied on a presumption of cosmic order, so construed that questions of the meaning, reason, purpose, function and cause of things all came together. Hence there were moral truths to be discerned by scientific understanding, including truths about human nature and our place in the cosmos at large. This moral knowledge had to do with an attunement to nature which could be achieved by practical reasoning based on grasp of the order of things – by practical wisdom, in short. By contrast, the idea of method and knowledge at the core of the scientific revolution fractured the old equation of meaning, reason, purpose, function and cause. Modern science deals only in causes, functions and biological purposes, whereas moral purposes, cosmic reasons and the meaning of life are none of its business. Although this divorce was only gradual and is not accepted by everyone even now, it was taking shape by the late eighteenth century, in the form of a 'deist compromise' which gave questions of causation to science and questions of meaning to religion.

But some *philosophes*, including Condorcet, presumed that God's purposes could be transferred to nature. They expected the advance of science to blow away all forms of superstition, thus clearing the way for an ethics which would be objective, because scientifically grounded in a true story about human nature. Condorcet, for instance, wrote that from man's ability to form and combine ideas 'there arise between him and his fellow creatures ties of interest and of duty, to which nature herself has wished to attach the most precious portion of our happiness and the most painful of our ills'.[2] Hume and Kant realised, however, that an external fabric of cosmic moral order could not be so simply replaced. Hume took the view that, starting from human nature, only a modest exercise was possible, a programme of identifying our natural sentiments, deciding which of them were useful to us and working out how best to cultivate them and discourage those which were not. It is true that here (and in Hobbes) lie the origins of the science of human welfare which Bentham tried to conjure up with the aid of the theory of utility, thus setting the tone for our manoeuvres on behalf of prudence. But, as noted, Hume's account of the passions does not encourage such ambitions.

2. Quoted in chapter 1 on p. 7.

Kant abandoned a naturalism resting on human nature and made it a general requirement of rationality that a rational being always acts on a maxim which universalises for all similar cases. Within his general account of practical reason, he distinguished the categorical imperative, whose demands on a rational agent are regardless of desires and consequences, from hypothetical imperatives of the form: 'If you want *x*, do *y*.' The latter operate under licence, so to speak, being permissions which are revoked if doing *y* would breach the demands of morality. Although metaphysically based in the nature of rational beings, Kantian practical reason can be presented as a formal answer *a priori* to such questions as 'What is it to act morally?' or 'What makes a rule a moral rule?' and so as an exercise in the logic of moral conduct. This formal aspect suits political theorists, who take Kant's *Rechtsstaat* as the formal political application of his notion of a 'kingdom of ends' for autonomous moral beings and hence an ideal framework for liberal ideas about human rights and liberties. It goes nicely with a distinction between the (formally) right and the (substantively) good.

Kantians and utilitarians attempt a rational ethics done without invoking an external cosmic order. Neither can hope to succeed if reason is equated with instrumental rationality, thus putting questions of the rationality of ends out of court. An associated fact/value distinction would then block rational access to a universal and moral point of view. Although philosophers in the Enlightenment line need not take the fact/value distinction lying down, they must be clear how they propose to dispute it. There is indeed Nietzsche's threat of paradox about the idea of an animal capable of promising – 'the paradoxical task which nature has set herself with mankind, the peculiar problem of mankind'. Kantian practical reason lifts the threat by rejecting naturalism, so as to let maxims alone be a motive to actions of the will. If this is artifice, it is not because an indirect strategy is artificial, when its licence is issued by the office of human welfare. The Kantian licence has no such source. But critics still deem it artificial to detach us morally from our inclinations and from all concern for consequences. Although defenders retort that the *Critique of Practical*

Reason can answer all questions about motivation, it is tempting to look for a more natural basis.

Utilitarian solutions accord with nature, in that they originate in the passions, advance by way of the moral sentiments and try to show that the acceptance of obligations is rational from the standpoint of overall utility. This last point may seem a specialty of Rule-utilitarians, with their all-but-Kantian account of duties as an artifice for the sake of better consequences. That makes them especially vulnerable to examples where the consequences of, for instance, breaking a promise are suboptimal. Their dilemma is that if they recommend sticking to principle regardless of consequences, then they are no longer utilitarians, and if not, then the artifice fails. But Act-, Motive- and any other forms of utilitarianism are not spared the dilemma, since they too are engaged in an artificial exercise to get philosophical egoists to adopt an impartial standpoint. An underlying philosophical egoism means starting with utility-for-one and prevents any smooth and logical transition from consequences for the particular agent to consequences for humanity at large. Naturalists have yet to deal with Hume's comment that our natural sentiments, being partial to ourselves, cannot yield an impartial point of view.

CONTRACTARIANS

In searching for remedies in the judgement and understanding for the untrustworthiness of the affections, rational ethics thus tends to fall between nature and artifice. But hope springs eternal and attempts to blend the two solutions continue. The remedies currently in favour are contractarian.

In *A Theory of Justice* John Rawls makes justice the bond of society, giving it enough of a moral quality to bind *in foro interno*. 'Justice is the first virtue of institutions', he remarks in the opening chapter whose title, 'Justice as fairness', sums up the idea pervading the book. The aim is to persuade rational egoists that they would subscribe to just institutions in their own self-interest if they did not know whether or not this would work out to their own advantage. Rational, self-interested individuals, he argues, if placed behind 'a veil of ignorance' which hid their particular strengths, weaknesses and place in history, would agree to a blend of Kantian and utilitarian precepts. They would bargain until they arrived at a reflective equilibrium embodying two broad principles of justice. These are, as stated in final form:

> First principle – Each person to have an equal right to the most extensive total system of equal basic liberties compatible with a similar system of liberty for all.
>
> Second principle – Social and economic equalities are to be arranged so that they are both:
>   (a) to the greatest benefit of the least advantaged, and
>   (b) attached to offices and positions open to all under conditions of fair equality of opportunity.[3]

The first or 'liberty' principle constrains the second, since no differences can be permitted, however great their welfare attraction, if they breach the scheme of maximal equal liberties.

These principles of justice as fairness are upheld in later versions, where the idea of a just society is glossed as 'a fair system of cooperation between free and equal persons'.[4] The phrase is a sort of portmanteau for some finely balanced Rawlsian claims. *Fairness* is a procedural notion, falling only a hair's breadth short of implying a thick conception of the good. *Cooperation* involves a notion of proper conduct Kantian enough to debar free-riding, yet, since a just society is an association of individuals, without requiring a collective moral purpose. The *freedom* envisaged leaves room for dispute over the merits of negative and positive versions between disciples of Locke (the 'moderns') and disciples of Rousseau (the 'ancients'). *Equality* constrains the distribution of power and resources without conceding to egalitarians. *Persons* are individuals who are essentially participants in social life, equipped with a capacity for a sense of justice and of the good; yet this conception does not call for a metaphysical doctrine of the nature of the self. These careful nuances mark a shift not

---

3. *A Theory of Justice*, Cambridge, Mass.: Harvard University Press, 1971, p. 302.
4. 'Justice as fairness: political not metaphysical', *Philosophy and Public Affairs*, 14 (1985), pp. 223–51, revised as chapter 1 of *Political Liberalism*, New York: Columbia University Press, 1993. The phrase occurs on p. 238 of the former and pp. 9 and 26 of the latter.

in the principles of justice recommended but in the basis of their appeal.

Rawls offers two ways to think about justice as fairness, instructively different for the basis of trust. The first, in part 1 of *A Theory of Justice*, is a matter of what would command the assent of ideally rational self-interested agents choosing a constitution behind 'a veil of ignorance'. Granted that they were suitably risk-averse, they would play safe and vote for arrangements which would suit them if they found themselves to be ill-favoured when the veil of ignorance came to be lifted. Morality is, so to speak, the best all-risks insurance policy for the unborn. Suppose that Adam did not yet know whether he would find himself to be rich or poor, clever or stupid, healthy or feeble, gay or straight. Then he would do well to vote for social arrangements which would suit him, whatever turned out to be the case. He would be rational, in short, to adopt the point of view of an impartial spectator which, when filled out, is seen to be the (Kantian) moral point of view, as embodied in a liberal *Rechtsstaat*. Adam and Eve, as they embark on the Enlightenment Trail, thus seem to have a neat solution to their problem. Let the game be between two players with preferences as previously stated and let the rules of the game be as before; but do not let Adam and Eve yet know which set of preferences is whose or who is to get first call. The best policy for each is then to agree to a cooperative strategy. Each rationally settles for a fair cooperation between free and equal persons by undertaking to keep on going all the way to The Triumph of Reason.

Does this show how it can be rational for Eve to trust Adam to pass up The Extra Trick? For reasons already given, I fear not. There is, alas, a sleight of hand in the equation of conveniently ignorant utility-maximisers with autonomous moral agents. It is exposed when the veil is lifted and the problem of compliance arises. Autonomous Kantians will then do what they have agreed to do, without regard to their own particular preferences or other consequential considerations. Utility-maximisers, by contrast, having acquired some very relevant further information, will set about hunting for bargains. Admittedly, you will not normally choose to take advantage of your strength, because you need my cooperation and have already helped to erect the scheme which turns out to protect me. So there will still be constraints. But, since rational maximisers never were Kantians, except extensionally in freak conditions, it is no surprise if they do not act like Kantians in other circumstances. Why, rationally speaking, should they? Admittedly too, Rawls, foreseeing this snag, equipped his constitution-makers with a 'purely formal' sense of justice which ensures that they expect to conform to the rules which they vote for (p. 145). But slipping a sense of justice, thin or thick, in among native sentiments is a dodge and, given Hume's reasons for calling justice an artificial virtue, too flimsy to withstand a consistent maximiser. Without it, however, the demands of mutual self-interest will not be congruent with those of the categorical imperative.

Rawls comes close to granting this, I think, in trying a different basis in *Political Liberalism*. In the earlier book he had offered what he called a 'conception' of justice, a contender in a competition to define the one and only true 'concept' of justice. The spirit was reminiscent of a Platonic dialogue seeking a true form amid conflicting definitions and ways of talking. The idea of 'justice as fairness' emerged as the truth of the matter, with justice a procedural notion which yields rules of association to suit self-interested persons without foreclosing on how they should conceive or live the good life. That version of the theory involved a good deal of what he termed 'metaphysics', especially in its view of the self in relation to its ends. *Political Liberalism* presents its theory of justice very differently. It is framed to apply not eternally or even universally but to the basic, consensual structure of a modern political democracy. It 'starts from within a particular political tradition', roughly the one which emerged in Western Europe from the wars of religion and which has established an 'overlapping consensus' about the virtues required of citizens as a basis for a historical construct.[5] Although the principles of justice are unchanged, the basis of their acceptance has become, as the subtitle of the intervening article claims, 'Political not metaphysical'.

5. 'Justice as fairness', p. 225, and *Political Liberalism*, pp. 14–15.

A true conception of justice might imply that obligations bind just because they have been undertaken. A conception relying on historical consensus does not. This is plainest where some members of a late twentieth-century plural culture refuse to accept that membership implies what liberals say about how the life of subcultures is to be conducted, for instance with equality of the sexes. But, even where consensus includes an apparent agreement that everyone should comply, we can still ask what underpins it. If the basis is still mutual self-interest, the question is still why rational persons are (morally?) bound to keep their covenants on occasions when prudence advises otherwise. If the basis is sheer history reinforced by politics, we are beyond the pale of Enlightenment reason. If a notion of reflective equilibrium is supposed to bridge the gap, we can only wonder how it can inject a binding element into a historical and political solution. That simply raises the original problem over again.

The most thorough attempt to equate morality with enlightened self-interest among instrumentally rational utility-maximisers is made by David Gauthier. In *Morals by Agreement* he divides rational agents into two sorts.[6] One the one hand there are 'straightforward maximisers', who always snap up a better bargain. These characters are exactly like Adam and Eve as first introduced, unable to resist the lure of a dominant logic and thus stuck at the very first pub on the Enlightenment Trail. They always defect in the Prisoner's Dilemma and never give a sucker an even break. So they all end up losers in the crucial situations; and serve them right! On the other hand, there are 'constrained maximisers', who are less foolish. Their moral psychology includes a disposition to play fair with those who play fair with them. They acquire this disposition by reflecting how much better they would do for themselves if they had it. But, lest they be made suckers, they do not practise it when dealing with straightforward maximisers. The enlightening idea is thus that it pays to be moral but only when dealing with others who agree that it pays to be moral when dealing with them in return.

6. David Gauthier, *Morals by Agreement*, Oxford University Press, 1986.

Like Rawls, Gauthier combines Kantian ethics and practical reasoning with a concern for consequences. Also like Rawls, he sets out to persuade rational egoists that self-interest is better served by adopting a shared moral point of view. The twist is a different way of tackling the problem of compliance. Gauthier's rational agents do not operate behind a veil of ignorance. They know who they are, what they possess by way of qualities and goods and where they stand in their social world. Yet they still find that it pays to play fair, although only with those who play fair with them. That is the basic idea and, after long and intricate argument, the upshot is supposedly a humanitarian ethics, resting on enlightened self-interest and crowned with a final uplifting chapter titled 'The liberal individual'. In formal proof of the pudding, Gauthier claims to have proved that constrained maximisers will cooperate even in a one-shot Prisoner's Dilemma and he would undoubtedly expect Adam and Eve to reach The Triumph of Reason.

An instructive implication of playing these games without a veil of ignorance is that, politically, Gauthier's agents are often libertarian where Rawls' are liberal. For example, he endorses no difference principle favouring the least well off and no other redistributive principle which might lead to a welfare state. When we ask why not, the theory starts to show a less humanitarian face. If Adam and Eve are both rich and strong, it may pay them to play one another fair. But what if Adam is rich and strong, whereas Eve is poor and weak? Given a theory resting squarely on the self-interest of people who already know their strengths, I cannot see why it pays him to be scrupulous. Even if the theory can show why it pays the strong to play fair with the strong, and the weak to play fair with the weak, what reason have the strong to play fair with the weak? The strong, I fancy, will rationally subscribe to only as much of a welfare state as they think a useful insurance policy for themselves. Lacking the self-interested sort of reason to go further provided by Rawls' veil of ignorance, they drive hard bargains with those in a weak bargaining position.

The strong do have an interest in keeping the weak in line and that may include greater welfare provision than they will make use of themselves. But provision made for losers in this spirit is more grudging than Rawls', granted that a veil of ignorance injects a mildly communitarian sense that we are all in the same boat. Gauthier's agents have no all-embracing communitarian spirit whatever. Indeed, it is not even as if each of the strong has an interest in playing fair with all the strong. Cartels are often a better option. What one individual cannot get away with can become very possible for a group of individuals, like a drug-dealers' ring, a hidden power-elite in a small town or a branch of the Mafia in a local setting. Provided that there can be honour among thieves, I see no reason whatever why a contractarian theory whose readers include the powerful and cunning should lead to the humanitarian, liberal morality which Gauthier asks us to agree to.[7]

Meanwhile a snag from our earlier discussion of moral psychology resurfaces. A constrained maximiser plays fair with some people and not with others. So the disposition to play fair can be switched on and off. It is Kantian in the On position and self-interestedly consequentialist in the Off. That requires a complex psychology with an agent who is at a distance from the switch and can decide whether to turn it on or off. Since this higher-order decision is to be taken on grounds of self-interest at a level where philosophical egoism is still in force, the earlier conundrum still awaits: how to flesh out a moral psychology where the agent can suspend forward-looking reasons for action, so as to act on Kantian maxims for the sake of improved consequences. This remains thoroughly awkward, especially given what was said earlier about steadfastness.

If these admittedly sketchy remarks are on target, Kant cannot be hitched to a contractarian wagon in the name of enlightened mutual self-interest. Contractarians are consequentialists who adopt a moral point of view as a device. However they then try to entrench it, it remains rational to suspend the device when better consequences are on offer. Hence self-interested individuals are not congruent with Kant's autonomous individuals. Autonomy goes with adopting the

---

7. For further discussion see my 'Honour among thieves' in *Reason in Action*, Cambridge University Press, 1996, and 'The agriculture of the mind' in D. Gauthier and R. Sugden (eds.), *Rationality, Justice and the Social Contract*, Hemel Hempstead: Harvester Wheatsheaf, 1993.

moral point of view regardless and eschews all substitutes for the genuine article.

MORALITY IN TRUST

So shall we conclude that the problem of trust can be solved by adopting Kant but only if we adopt him wholesale? Since Kantians would indeed reach The Triumph of Reason, this is not an unattractive conclusion. They can be trusted to keep promises and agreements, and, in so far as the missing element in trust is a moral bond, Adam and Eve will do well to be guided by *The Critique of Practical Reason*. At any rate, it has emerged, I submit, that any moral element in trust needs to be the genuine article and not just an ingenious remedy for a myopia endemic in philosophical egoists.

But it is not yet clear whether the crux is a notion of rationality other than an instrumental one or a shift to a moral point of view or both. The emerging story about rationality goes like this. We presumed at first that to call an action rational is to endorse the agent's choice of the means to a given end, namely the furthering of an existing desire or interest. The fact/value distinction then seemed to block any question of the rationality of ends, provided that the agent's desires are coherent and realistic. So the problem seemed to be one of making rational sense of disputes about the rationality of ends and its solution a matter of showing that moral reasoning is a form, or perhaps the ideal-type, of practical reason. This seems to me a possible way to go. Kant is undaunted by the fact/value distinction; and Kantian practical reason gives people rational guidance about what they should do, without appealing to an external moral cosmos. He insists that, in acting on a maxim which passes muster from the moral point of view, one is acting rationally. Where moral considerations do not apply, instrumental reasons come into play, as, for instance, with the rational way to mend a fuse safely. But instrumental reasons are trumped by moral reasons in cases where both are relevant. Kant would give me no marks for rational conduct in mending the fuse in my wife's hair-drier safely if my reason was to electrocute her by dropping the gadget into her bath. This strikes me as right and it implies

that reasons for action are, or can be, external to the agent's desires and
beliefs.

The crucial move, however, is not a bridging of the fact / value distinction in hope of deriving 'ought' from 'is', but the claim that to act
rationally is to adopt a universal standpoint. Prudence might wish to
recommend such a standpoint but was unable to do so. (The earlier
arguments will be reinforced when we discuss joint action further in
chapter 7.) To focus the issue, here is another little game, which might
be called 'The Common Good'.

		Eve	
		X	Y
Adam	X	1, 1	0, 1
	Y	1, 0	0, 0

The Common Good

Here Adam's pay-off depends wholly on what Eve chooses and *vice
versa*. So neither has any game-theoretic reason to prefer X to Y (or Y to
X). Each is, formally speaking, indifferent and any choice is an equally
rational choice. Yet, if they could only view the game from a collective
angle, they could not fail to see that XX gets them 1 each. But, as far as I
can see, there is no way for prudence to make this a relevant considera-
tion. X would be a more rational choice than Y only if it had a higher
expected utility and here it does not. One might suggest playing X on
the grounds that it makes (1,1) possible, whereas Y makes a gloomy
(0,0) possible. But this simply cuts no ice, while Adam is guided only by
his pay-off and Eve only by hers. The possibility of collective action in
pursuit of a *common* good eludes them.

The puzzle cries out for Adam and Eve to play as a team, a partnership whose collective aim is the common good of the partners.
Moreover, this would be a rational way to play, if rationality were universal before it was particular. That was what Hume's remedy requires
and Smith's impartial spectator might suggest, but without success

while teams are sums of separate individuals. Does the idea that a rational agent always acts on a universal maxim do the trick? Yes, it does, in the sense that a maxim directing everyone to the common good succeeds if obeyed by all. But it remains unclear why the solution is not simply *ad hoc*, given the initial definition of rationality. Appeal to a universal standpoint answers the objection by claiming that the initial definition was wrong. But that simply shifts the question to the basis of the new one. A stand-off now occurs. Why should Eve adopt the standpoint of the common good? A ready answer is 'because she will do better for herself thereby'. But this answer is open to the objection that, if unconditional, it is false. *She* does better only if *he* adopts that standpoint; and, if he does, she still has no reason to do likewise. The right answer has to be 'because the common good is the standpoint implicit in practical reason'. But that is precisely what is in question.

I see two possible ways to end the stand-off. One is a radical challenge to the individualism assumed so far, to be tried in the next chapter. The other is to make explicit the moral theory which contractarianism has been vainly trying to harness to the chariot of prudence, thus resuming the thought that any morality inherent in trust needs to be the genuine article. The strong Kantian links between rationality, autonomy and morality remain enticing. But I do not believe that the moral element in trust is finally of a Kantian character, because the bond of society is more conditional and strategic than an analysis stemming from the categorical imperative will countenance. I recognise, however, that better Kant scholars than I may want to resist the next few paragraphs.

What makes Kantians trustworthy is their unswerving determination to act from duty, regardless of what anyone else may be up to. Trust, as the *vinculum societatis*, seems to me more defeasible. For instance, it used to be common in Britain to leave the doors to one's house unlocked, so that friends, neighbours and people like plumbers, with business to be there, could get in. It was a useful habit, especially for the housebound, and it is sad to see it going. But, as local crime has increased, this habit of trust has retreated from loose-knit neighbourhoods to tight-knit ones and from towns to country villages. The withdrawal shows that it was a conditional trust and, even in its heyday, dependent on neighbours knowing one another's affairs and keeping an eye open. Yet it also expressed a moral view of neighbourliness and the sanctity of people's homes and property. This view made it rational – or should I say 'reasonable'? – to leave doors unlocked, provided that the trust was reciprocated. It ceased to be so, as breaches grew common.

I offer this as a small example of a norm which has a genuine moral content but is not plausibly construed as a universal maxim. Even if there is a potential maxim in 'Respect the property of others', it is grounded in particular social relations, rather than a set of unconditional imperatives from which social relations can be derived. The categorical imperative is sometimes loosely stated as 'Do as you would be done by.' This is a mistake, since how you *want* people to treat you depends on what sort of person you happen to be and what you happen to want. Even 'Do as you *should* be done by' does not catch the Kantian rule, if it suggests that you need not be so high-minded when others do not treat you properly. This, however, is exactly what defeasible relations of trust seem to me to involve. They are strategic, in the sense that how trusting one is required to be depends on how trustworthy others are.

Kantians can reply that, although they are unswerving in doing their duty, they are also flexible in deciding what their duty is. A maxim which applies to Britain in 1960 may not do so forty years on, since situations superficially alike can be relevantly different. Hence it is misleading to say that Kantians act regardless of what others are up to. They are under no obligation to leave doors unlocked for the benefit of friends in a world full of burglars. If 'Leave your door open' is a universal maxim which fails, 'Leave your door locked' is not the only alternative. There is also 'Leave your door open unless there are burglars about.' Being therefore a hypothetical case, it does not embarrass the categorical imperative.

That reply sounds right but sets a familiar question about the line between hypothetical and categorical imperatives. A maxim about telling the truth, for example, is not to be set aside because the Gestapo asks the whereabouts of one's Jewish friends. I think that Kantian practical reason is high-minded as well as practical and its practitioners must expect to get their fingers burnt from time to time through acting morally in a world which they know to be imperfect. Hence, a maxim bidding us tell the truth is not to be so heavily qualified that we have no such duty when dealing with the wicked, or even, to slip further down the slope, have a duty to tell them lies. When the Gestapo asks Kantians where their Jewish friends are hiding, a serious problem is set. For, even if 'Tell lies' cannot be universalised, 'Tell lies to the wicked' can be; but Kantians cannot adopt it. Hence Kantian flexibility stops short of reintroducing strategic choice into the whole business of trust; yet it is not plain where flexibility stops, or where exactly runs the boundary between Kantian reason's practicality and its high-mindedness.

Meanwhile it is worth checking whether disingenuous maxims reinstate the block on the Enlightenment Trail. Does the maxim which made Adam and Eve trustworthy say 'Aim for the common good' or 'Aim for the common good, when interacting with people who aim for the common good'? The latter maxim is indeed universal but does not do the job required. My tentative conclusion is that Kantians can be flexible only within a rigid frame, thus getting the wrong measure of the way in which trust is defeasible. Their morality has to be too high-minded to serve as the bond of society. The conclusion is tentative, because Kant has much to say on related matters and I have confined myself to one topic. Nevertheless, I shall chance my arm further with a remark about duty and inclination, before broaching the promised challenge to individualism in the next chapter.

The trust involved in leaving the door unlocked is not to do with fair play, I suspect, even duty-driven fair play. There is a moral element, but not one related to a belief that people's sense of duty will overcome their desire to take advantage of an unlocked door. That would belie the idea of neighbourliness which informs relations among neighbours. This is an elusive remark, whose point may be clearer from an example suggested by Rüdiger Bittner. When Eve is ill in hospital, she has visitors who come to cheer her up. Among them are Kantians, who come because they ought to, not from motives of love, pity or pleasure in her company but because of a maxim about hospital-visiting. Since they will do her more good if she thinks that they come for her sake and from those motives, they may be careful to give that impression. But Eve, suspecting this, does not trust them, not because they are not upright but because they are moved by the wrong sort of motive. Their respect for all persons fails to be respect for her in particular.

This example hints at a different idea of morality, grounded in personal ties and particularised social relations. The hint will be taken up in the next chapter.

Conclusion

Our attempts on the problem of trust so far have conceived Adam, Eve and all of us as socially abstracted individuals. This was overt in the starting point, where the artificial, game-theoretic setting highlighted their separation from each other by abstracting them from all social context. It then carried over to more everyday examples of the problem, where we still found fleshlier Adams and Eves treating social relations as instrumental in the pursuit of their separate individual ends. That was due to the pervasive philosophical egoism built into the desire/belief model of action, as expressed in the thesis that only Adam's desires can move Adam and that only Eve's can move Eve.

The injection of more amiable passions, starting with sympathy, did not challenge this version of individualism, nor did a detour through parts of the theory of the social contract. Indeed the versions proposed in *A Theory of Justice* and *Morals by Agreement* were explicit in their reliance on it. In Rawls' words, 'the self is prior to the ends which are affirmed by it'.[8] That is hardly surprising if society is seen as an association of individuals and the social contract as a device made rational by mutual self-interest. But it is no less true of the moral point of view, treated as the genuine Kantian article and as a source of

8. *A Theory of Justice*, p. 560.

reasons for actions done solely because they are right. Indeed Kantian autonomy is precisely a celebration of the moral dimension of Kantian individualism.

As noted, what makes Kantians trustworthy is their unswerving determination to act from duty, regardless of what anyone else may or may not be up to. It is not their relationship with other people, except in so far as they treat others as ends in themselves and refrain from exploiting them. In this highly abstract scheme people recognise one another as selves distinct from their human and social peculiarities and treat one another impersonally and fairly, as required by the universal maxims which guide moral action. It does the trick and makes them trustworthy but, I surmise, not in a way which reveals the secret of trust.

What does? In the next chapter I shall rummage deeper in the magician's hat and argue that we need a more social conception of what persons are and a role-related account of the obligations which make the social world go round and express our humanity.

6
All in the game

The problem of trust lies in what Kant termed 'man's asocial sociality'.[1] If we were wholly asocial, there would be no trust; if wholly social, no problem. Since we have both elements, however, we need to decide how elastic to make the bond of society. Is it one which adapts to who we are and where we belong? This would be a plausible answer if the question were solely one of who does in practice trust whom. But it is not an answer within reason to an Enlightenment question of who merits trust. That may yet turn out to be a moral question requiring the moral answer that only those who act uprightly should be trusted. But, if this implies a Kantian moral point of view, its universalising character is double-edged. It shows how trustworthy persons can overcome the perils of prudence and reach The Triumph of Reason. But it does so by making each so unconditionally moral that progress along the trail does not depend on trust at all. Hence it neither captures the conditional character of everyday trust nor lets us ask which social relations generate trust-within-reason.

1. 'Idea for a universal history with a cosmopolitan purpose' (1784), 4th Proposition, in *Kant's Political Writings*, ed. Hans Reiss, trans. H. B. Nisbet, Cambridge University Press, 1970.

Reason grants that one can find many examples of trust, as in honour among thieves, teamwork among terrorists and a shared sense of mission among missionaries. It does not grant that these are all examples of trust-within-reason, however, and we need to know which, if any, it approves. To ask, we must explore the idea that we are more embedded in social relations than modern individualists usually allow. So, after a prelude describing the current state of play in the Enlightenment soccer league, the chapter will deploy some Wittgensteinian thoughts about the games of social life. It will then ask about the players of these games, sharpening the question with the aid of the 'dramaturgical analogy'. A case will emerge for saying that people are social before they are individual, and plural before they are singular. It may extend to making obligation internal to local practices. But, however enticing this idea of *Sittlichkeit*, it does not offer a solution to the problem of trust-within-reason and the chapter will end still seeking a critical and universal standpoint.

PRELUDE: ENLIGHTENMENT FOOTBALL

Albert Camus once played soccer for Algeria. I learnt this not from *The Outsider*, *The Fall* or his other contributions to philosophy, but from a tee-shirt emblazoned in gold letters with the legend: 'All that I know most surely about morality and obligations I owe to football. (Albert Camus).' So let us try a more athletic approach to truth, virtue and happiness. Soccer, played in the right spirit, is a team game involving trust, obligations and a willingness to play fair. Since we have concentrated so far on individuals, we have not yet thought much about teams. To start us off, here is a sketch of three teams from the Enlightenment football league, whose fortunes are instructively varied.

Bottom of the league at present are the Marketeers, a side of rampant individualists, each of whom is out to score as many goals as possible. That may sound a very practical attitude, since the more goals each scores, the better the team does. Unfortunately, however, each player's primary aim is to score goals himself. This has been spurred by the team's new manager, who decided to stimulate the team and encourage star players with an offer of a large personal bonus to every scorer of a goal. The effect was immediate. The players became so keen to score that they stopped passing the ball until blocked by opponents and then did so only if they expected to get it back shortly. Otherwise they preferred to kick it out of play, in hope of regaining it from the throw in. The results were predictably catastrophic. Even the star players failed to score, since they got the ball no more often than anyone else, and the team was soon losing every match.

So the manager next set about persuading the players that there was mutual advantage to be had from passing the ball, not merely when one expected to get it back oneself but also in a more general spirit of reciprocity. This had some effect. Bilateral exchanges began to yield to multilateral and a norm of passing emerged, which meant that the Marketeers started to score a few goals. But, given the bonus system, the norm was precarious, since players continued to grab chances for scoring themselves, even when passing meant a higher chance of someone else scoring. Worse, the goalkeeper and backs became mutinous and insisted on trying to score goals themselves. This left the goal wide open; and matters did not improve when the manager introduced a new bonus for each goal saved. That merely had the defenders getting in one another's way. Since he is now out of fresh ideas and team spirit is an alien concept for individualists, the Marketeers are doomed to stay at the bottom of the league.[2]

Half way up the league at present are Königsberg Universal. Their attitude is very different. Players who get the ball ask themselves what any and every player so placed should do with it, and, thus armed with a universal maxim, act accordingly. When duty says 'Shoot', they shoot. When duty says 'Pass', they pass; and the ball finds team mates correctly positioned, since they too have been performing correlative exercises in practical reasoning. Since each player can trust the others completely, Königsberg Universal is faring better than the Marketeers.

2. Relatedly, all economic enterprises need to count on more loyalty from their members than fear or money can buy. If an 'economic' solution to the problem of trust does not work in general, it does not work for markets, which quickly collapse without a fiduciary element.

But there are drawbacks to so high-minded a style of play. An initial one was that it used to take time to identify the relevant maxim and by then opponents had collared the ball. This has since been overcome by practice – a case where habit is not the enemy but the friend of reason. The major one remains, however, that the players are unclear how much regard to have for consequences. They soon discovered that, if maxims are kept simple – 'Shoot, whenever in the penalty area' – and applied unswervingly, opponents too often get in the way. But the corrective is tricky, since maxims which pack in too many clauses about what the opposition might do are unworkable, and anyway are, arguably, too concerned with consequences to serve as maxims.

The team has discussed treating the game as a matter of hypothetical imperatives, rather than categorical. But they have decided that football is too important and too definitely requires that they treat one another as autonomous. So they have had to settle for a style of play which is admirable in each player, considered singly, and sometimes achieves the harmony of a fully rehearsed orchestra but fails against teams who do not care about the ethics or aesthetics of the game. They are therefore resigned to a place in the middle of the league, consoled by the thought that autonomous players respect one another's autonomy too much for complete worldly success.

Top of the league at present are the Musketeers, a close-knit team whose motto is 'All for one and one for all'. Each Musketeer is self-effacing to the point where only the team matters. Even their more swashbuckling manoeuvres give them pleasure solely because this glorious style of play brings goals, fame and honour to the team. They take pride in their play but not a self-glorifying pride, and no one ever swashes a buckle when it would be nobler to pass the ball. They worship their team with a collective loyalty which crushes all individuality. The Musketeers are thus victorious; but not solely because they are stylish or, indeed, even sporting. Their determination to win is fired by a conviction that their opponents are there to be beaten. So, although they respect teams like themselves and play with gallantry in those matches, they otherwise play as rough as the rules permit. Their sense of obligation to one another and to the game itself does not extend to what they regard as outsiders, in short, and they have no sense of the fun of the game.

Of the three teams, the Musketeers come closest so far to illuminating the bond of society, I think. The sort of obligation among them is neither the Marketeers' fragile gum of mutual self-interest nor the categorical superglue which keeps the Königsberg players rigidly upright in treating one another (and their opponents) as ends in themselves. Obligation among Musketeers derives from complete identification with their particular team. But, although this makes for success on the field, it does so because other teams are trapped in philosophies which make for poor football and so do not truly put the Musketeers to the test. When we ask what exactly makes them animals capable of promising, some previous questions resurface. 'Complete identification' can be taken in two ways. It could mean simply that what each Musketeer wants most is for the team to do well and, to this end, therefore wants trust to flourish among them. Then, despite their flaunting of the team's livery, their waxed moustachios and lace-embroidered cuffs, they are still individualists at heart and one wonders how they came to have self-effacing preferences. Since they were not born with an innate and overriding team spirit, did they choose their preferences by a novel trick of their moral psychology? That seems impossible, because an individualist who is a philosophical egoist can neither have an internal reason to cease being one nor be moved by an external reason, and an individualist who is not a philosophical egoist can, so far, only be a Kantian.

Alternatively 'complete identification' might mean that, having somehow imbibed musketeering as a way of life, they obey the norms which put their team first blindly and untroubled by critical doubt. It never troubles them, for instance, that the loyalty which gives them their collective strength is essentially bound up with contempt for outsiders. They are, in some ways, more like ants obedient to the demands of the ant colony than humans intelligent about the values which inform their lives. So, although their word is their bond, in that their loyalty to the team and to each other is total, there is an unobvious question whether they are truly animals capable of promising. They are too blindly and bone-headedly obedient to the demands of norms which are solely for the benefit of the team. Do they really understand what it is to be bound by one's word? Are they never tempted to break a promise? What dilemmas do they experience? The Musketeers do not provide answers to these questions.

This is as far as a prelude can take us. But the questions stand. Is it finally possible to be an individual who puts the team first? That sounds like a contradiction in terms. But we might try thinking of such individuals as philosophical egoists with preferences which measure consequences by the benefit to the team, or as Kantians with less than universal commitments. Perhaps there can be a team of such players, yet to enter the league but destined for the top. In that case what Camus gained from football was precisely a grasp of morality and obligations. But, if so, the Enlightenment Trail grows difficult indeed and we shall have to think through what an Enlightenment version of asocial sociality involves.

Meanwhile, football is also instructive in a different way. Being a game in the everyday sense, it contrasts notably with 'games' as defined by game theory. That suggests a different way to construe the fertile thought that social life consists of the games people play. The next phase of this chapter will explore the idea that the self is socially embedded by thinking some Wittgensteinian thoughts about action as an expression of rules and meanings.

THE GAMES OF SOCIAL LIFE

Think first about team games and membership of teams. Football is to be understood in terms of rules, as distinct from regularities. It may or may not have evolved from a casual pastime for idle folk with a spare pig's bladder. By now, however, it has advanced from emergent habits to formal rules, which specify, for instance, what counts as a goal and as a win, loss or draw. Historically, the process was gradual but, analytically, its end is different in kind from its beginning. Some of the rules are constitutive, in the sense that they define the purpose of the game and thus create possibilities for action. This is not a matter of labelling actions which could have been be performed previously.

Since no goals could be scored before there were rules to define a goal, any earlier kicking of a bladder through a doorway was a different action. The constitutive rules are fleshed out with formal regulations, which translate the general purpose into detail, for instance rules governing when a player is offside and how a throw-in shall be taken. The difference between constitutive and formal regulative rules is not precise; but, roughly, the latter specify which exact form the game shall take among those consistent with the essentials defined by the former. One could, for example, vary the offside rule without the game's ceasing to be football.

This formal framework of constitutive and regulative rules has something to say about players, but only schematically. For instance, there shall be no more than eleven a side and only the goalkeeper may handle the ball; but the rules of the game neither require nor forbid strikers. Formal regulations thus shade into custom and habit. Yet, although not recognised formally, striker is an established position with a role attached which the incumbent is expected to play in a definite way. Roles are sets of expectations attached to social positions and, although also a predictive guide to what people are likely to do, such expectations are essentially normative. They come with a quasi-moral vocabulary of entitlement to performance, of praise for good play and of reproach for bad. There are degrees and sorts of normativity involved: a goalie *must* know the rules, *should* have a safe pair of hands and *can be looked to* for a brilliant save now and then. They all have shades of obligation not present in the notion of strategic predictability.

'Quasi-moral' is an uneasy term but I cannot readily do better. Serious football calls for meritorious skills and virtues. Had Aristotle lectured on football, he would have had much to say both about the proper function and character of goalkeepers and centre-forwards and about how these different *aretai* combine to make for an effective team and a satisfying game. The skills range from ball-control to intelligent anticipation, the virtues from loyalty and courage to generosity and sportsmanship. Some of these virtues are unpuzzlingly moral, whereas others are peculiar to the game and, indeed, morally peculiar. That may be clearer from other games of love and war, where all's fair and virtue explicitly includes dealing dirt to opponents as much as generosity to comrades. Expectations can be no less normative for being ethically dubious and 'quasi-moral' signals a notion of obligation which needs very careful thought.

Ancient Greece in Aristotle's time had not made sport commercial, even if the Olympic Games had brought political rivalry between city states to the innocence of contests between individual athletes. So Aristotle could have taken a high-minded view of the game and prescribed its virtues as good moral training for young citizens. But today's football is very big business and its positions and roles include many off the pitch. Directors, accountants and public relations experts have an idea of a satisfying game which can be calibrated in column inches and quantified at the box office. Whether this attendant circus belongs to the game of football is perhaps moot, but it is plainly part of the practice and institution. Within the larger realm, goalies may not always be expected to save goals, since it is not unknown for games to be fixed. On the other hand, such latent expectations depend on going undetected amid the contrary public expectations; and questions of what exactly is then meant by 'normative' become complex.

At any rate, football is not simply a game played for its own sake on a well-defined pitch, marked with white lines to show its boundaries. Its boundaries are wider than the pitch and we cannot understand the practice of football just by understanding its overt rules. There are more rules than the overt, more latitude in interpreting them and more in the minds of the players. Care is needed in drawing an analogy between literal games and social practices at large. Yet the very ambiguity about the line between what is internal and external to the game of football is helpful in thinking about the relation between teams and players. The Marketeers evidently do not lose their individuality when they take their places on the field, nor is their play intelligible if understood solely by reference to group norms expressed as requirements attached to each role in the team. Yet this is not because a Marketeer is an instance of *homo economicus,* and, more generally, one can think of any marketeer as *homo sociologicus,* a role-player in a market context. In any case, role-players should never be thought of as puppets who neither have nor need minds of their own. Even the Musketeers, who apparently rose to the top of the league by suppressing all individuality for the sake of obedience, do not want players who are slavishly and blindly obedient to the rules and the demands of victory. Mindlessness does not win matches. In short, the fertile Wittgensteinian analogy between games and social practices thus makes us think of people as participants by posing deep questions about the players who follow the rules. Yet the problem of trust does not simply vanish with the thought that embedded players can of course be trusted to do what is expected of them. They – and we, as social observers – still need to think in terms of latitude in interpreting the rules and perhaps of distance from them.

This emerges more clearly if we turn briefly to another well-tried analogy for understanding social life, where interpretation and distance are centre stage. Consider the dramaturgical analogy, which invites us to think of life as theatre. It proposes the idea that social actors play roles rather as dramatic actors play parts, an idea neatly captured by Jaques in *As You Like It*:

> All the world's a stage
> And all the men and women merely players.

Tantalisingly, however, this apothegm points in two directions. It seems at first to say that life consists of dramas whose scripts we did not write and in which we merely act out the characters provided for us. That need not imply that we are puppets in a puppet theatre rather than human actors in a live theatre. Live actors bring something of themselves to the script. They interpret it in their own way, or, granted the power of the director, at least influence the interpretation offered in a particular production. The leading actors have enough latitude to make Laurence Olivier's Hamlet almost a different character from Mel Gibson's. But the limits are severe. No one's Hamlet can answer the question 'To be or not to be?' by deciding that 'not to be' is the better consummation and run himself through with a bodkin. That would not do at all. Hence, if we are merely players, we still matter; but the script matters more.

On the other hand, actors are not identical with any single character played:

> They have their exits and their entrances
> And one man in his time plays many parts.

That suggests an actor, distinct from his many parts and donning and doffing them like masks. In each part, latitude in interpretation has severe limits; but, in the choice of parts which sum to a life, we have a latitude which makes us not the parts but their players. On this account, there is a self distinct from each and every role. The several scripts matter; but we matter more.

Yes, but where do the exits lead? If *all* the world's a stage, then an exit from one part is always an entrance into another, with backstage in one play always front stage in the next. It is not as if one's public life were a series of stages and one's private life not a stage at all. If *all* the world's a stage, so is the private sanctum, where only intimates are admitted. Indeed, if we follow the thought to its end, I am never alone with myself, because the self alone is but a shadow of a self on stage.

The dramaturgical analogy can thus be given two readings. In amateur theatricals, the self dons a mask for the occasion and pretends to be the character in that evening's play. I, who play the part and impersonate someone else, am a self distinct from my roles. In professional theatre, by contrast, the actor is a chameleon who personifies a character. I am the set of my characters and thus the hero in the drama of my own life – a sort of meta-play in which they all appear. That way of putting it makes the professional interpretation of the analogy seem the more profound. But it conceals a further ambiguity. Bill Clinton, in playing his presidential role, does not impersonate the President of the United States, since he *is* the President. Yet neither does he exactly personify the President, except in so far as he plays the President in a suitably presidential style. For, if men and women are *merely* players, then Bill Clinton is a role too and, although he does not pretend to be Bill Clinton, since that is who he is, neither does he personify a Bill Clinton who, on this account, does not exist as a distinct person or someone to be personified. In sum, the more thoroughly we

construe the dramaturgical analogy as saying that the self is a character in the play of its own life, the more complex and obscure it
becomes, until finally we can understand it only by understanding
what it is meant to illuminate.

Similarly, to draw a Wittgensteinian analogy between literal games
and the games or practices of social life is not to turn a spotlight on a
dark place. It is more like a candle, whose flickering suggestion is that
social realities are constructed by adopting constitutive meaning-
rules, which engender social positions and roles attended with normative expectations. But that does not settle questions of whether the
rules of the game dictate the action and whether we who play the
game are their creatures. The line is, more ambiguously, that rules
always enable as well as constrain and that, in both aspects, they
emerge by interpretation while also governing their interpreters. We,
the interpreters, belong to the social reality which we construct and, in
learning the rules, we become particular persons; yet we also stand
outside the construction, which is as we decide it shall be.

The analogy also has two striking implications. The first is that we
who construct the action are social beings before we are particular
individuals and are plural before we are singular. In a literal game, I can
make no actual moves unless there are possible moves to make, and so
unless there are rules already; and I can make my moves only if there
are other players who recognise what moves they are. Analogously, I,
as an individual, cannot mean anything by my action unless there is
something which my action means and other people to recognise that
this is what it does mean. Only within this social and plural space can I
have more private motives for doing what has this public meaning.
Press harder and perhaps my private motives turn out to be moves in
some further game, rather as, in the dramaturgical analogy, the exits
from one theatrical stage may always be entrances to another. If so,
there is no more a secret self than there is a private language.

The other implication is a gloss on 'quasi-moral': the morality of
action, like its meaning, is internal to context. 'Morality' is a double-
edged word to use but 'normativity' would be too bland. The obligation on a footballer to be unselfish about passing the ball or on a

researcher not to suppress unfavourable evidence is more than part of what one is paid for, even if it seems less than a pukka moral obligation. The ground here is treacherous. On the one hand, we are inclined to distinguish normative expectations from pukka moral obligations, since there are roles whose morality we would firmly deny. Thomas Nagel has remarked, 'I cannot acquire a duty to murder someone just by taking a job as hit-man for the Mafia.'[3] It would be hard to quarrel with that. Yet this is what hit-men are engaged to do and, internally speaking, failure to perform lays them open to righteous anger and a bullet for dishonourable conduct. *Mafiosi* are bound by an honour code, strict and efficacious, which keeps them loyal unto death or at least imprisonment. Recent work on the Mafia presents it as an unusual but profitable species of economic enterprise, in the business of marketing trust.[4] Were that the whole story, there would be the same puzzle about the Mafia as about loyalty within firms which operate in a market which they view as a jungle: why economic and instrumental relations with outsiders do not undermine relations of honour among insiders. Within the Mafia, presumably, *omertà* and other elements of the honour code are binding, as Hobbes would say, *in foro interno* as well as *in foro externo*. Although this becomes evidently puzzling if the prime purpose of the Mafia is economic, it is still puzzling if honour is primary among people who live in two worlds. Part of the problem is set by needing to use the term 'quasi-moral'. Internally speaking, I can indeed acquire a 'quasi-duty' to murder someone just by taking a job as a hit-man.

The Wittgensteinian suggestion that obligations are always internal to local practices makes us uneasy. But many institutions and practices depend on obligations which we must dub 'quasi-moral', whether or not we are willing to go further. A vendetta, for instance, can oblige your cousin to kill my cousin, even though these parties of

3. Thomas Nagel, 'Ruthlessness in public life', in S. Hampshire (ed.), *Public and Private Morality*, Cambridge University Press, 1978.
4. See especially Diego Gambetta, 'Mafia: the price of distrust', in D. Gambetta (ed.), *Trust: Making and Breaking Cooperative Relations*, Oxford: Basil Blackwell, 1988, pp. 158–75.

the third and fourth part had nothing to do with the original offence. The massacre of Glencoe, which took place in the Western Highlands of Scotland in 1692, still entitles Campbells and Macdonalds to distrust one another three hundred years later. There are still self-respecting Southerners who would not give a damned Yankee the time of day. Such examples tend to have feet uneasily planted both *in foro externo* and *in foro interno*. But they make a vital point about how 'quasi-duties' work. The bonds of clan, race, creed, class and gender often bind insiders in ways which are morally neither neutral nor, from an Enlightenment point of view, laudable. They often depend on a sense of belonging upheld by contempt for outsiders, who are treated as inferior or even as less than fully human.

This is one source of queasiness about the binding character of normative expectations. Commentators who fear that the spread of economic and technological rationality is destroying the social virtues and rotting the social fabric sometimes note with relief that there are forces resistant to it, like those of kinship, patriotism, nationalism and fundamentalist religion. Yes, but these forces, when untempered, can unite insiders by a sense of superiority to outsiders. Then they are dark forces, often dreadful in their effects and able to flourish only in the shadows where the light of reason does not reach. To rejoice in them indiscriminately is not a solution to the problem of trust which anyone on the Enlightenment Trail can accept.

REASON AND OBLIGATION

Yet there is something in these social ties to rejoice in, and so something amiss with any version of the Enlightenment project which puts them all beyond the pale of reason. To locate what is rational in practices which secure trust, however, and what is irrational or non-rational, we shall need a fresh notion of reason and of reasons for action. So far we have tried taking rationality first as calculation in the service of passions or preferences and secondly as deliberation conducted from the moral point of view. Since neither line has enlightened us about trust, the Wittgensteinian hints just dropped point to what sounds like a third and winning line, a notion of rationality as rule-following.

Let us cast it in terms of reason for action. Social actors follow rules, both constitutive and regulative, and these rules can provide reasons for action. The rules of chess or football provide the players with reasons which they would not otherwise have. The rules of social institutions do likewise for the players of roles, with examples ranging from parental reasons for teaching children manners, through the reasons which a Catholic priest has for remaining celibate or a Quaker for pacifism, to those which prompt *mafiosi* to kill people or cannibals to eat them.

There is at least one simple and strong argument in favour of inter-nalising reasons for action to the clusters of rules which social actors follow. It is that we can understand the practices which I have been taking as examples and the actions which are done accordingly. Understanding advances by finding rationality in what is understood, even if only in a weak sense. To understand what people are doing is, at least as a first step, to reconstruct their reasons for doing it. In so far as those reasons derive from the rules followed, reconstruction proceeds by identifying the rules of the game and shows how actions are thereby rendered rational. For instance, killing is not senseless if it is prescribed in the course of a vendetta to avenge a previous killing. If someone asks whether it is *truly* rational to kill for this reason, the question can be usefully deflected for the moment by taking it as a question either about whether the actor has correctly followed the rule or about how the practice relates to other practices. The question of what is truly rational then, no doubt, recurs. But, in so far as it is one about what makes any and every rule ultimately rational, it can be parried by remarking:

> Don't say: 'There *must* be something common, or they would not be called "games"' – but *look and see* whether there is anything common to all. For if you look at them you will not see something that is common to *all*, but similarities, relationships, and a whole series of them at that.[5]

If the questioner persists, however, the text allows the thought that looking and seeing presuppose a shared, universal framework or

5. L. Wittgenstein, *Philosophical Investigations*. Oxford: Basil Blackwell. 1953, I, para. 66.

bedrock. But it lies in very general facts of experience, more to do with our physical situation than with our cultural predispositions. If so, the stopper is not a final refusal to recognise reasons external to all practices but an insistence that final reasons, if statable at all, are not of a sort which yields specific cultural reasons. There is no simple cultural relativism about 'forms of life' in the lapidary view that

What has to be accepted, the given, is, so to say, *forms of life*.[6]

Nevertheless, as I read it, there is still an implication that *cultural* reasons are indeed relative to cultures, thus making the 'quasi-' element in 'quasi-morality' ineliminable.

From this angle, the problem of trust looks simple again. The players of most or even all games of social life can be counted on to follow the rules, since their actions are always essentially rule-governed. That makes them reliable in general, both predictively and normatively, and often reliable in precise ways also, owing to specific rules requiring trust and reciprocity. If these inferences are not sure-fire, it must be either because there is latitude in the interpretation of the relevant rules or because, with people usually playing several games at the same time, it is unclear which rules are relevant and crucial. It cannot be because people sometimes act not as rule-followers but, for instance, as rational economic individual utility maximisers, since market behaviour, like all other social behaviour, is rule-governed, with markets simply further examples of practices and institutions. In sum, it becomes rational to trust anyone following a rule which makes them reliable.

On reflection, however, this is muddled thinking. Its starting point seems right enough: we make sense of social action by reference to rules which work analogously to rules of a game; and the sense thus made must relate to the actors' own sense and so implies that they are guided by the rules of specific practices and institutions as they understand them. But the blocking moves in the two quotations above are too peremptory. The questioner who asks whether it is rational for a *mafioso* to shoot people or a cannibal to eat them may be asking for a

6. *Ibid.*, II, p. 226.

general criterion which discriminates between rational and irrational rules. In that case, it is part of an answer to remark that games do not have enough in common to permit such a general criterion and to add that specific questions must therefore be referred to specific practices. But what if the questioner refuses to accept that, even for cultural purposes, cultural forms of life must be accepted? It is all very well to advise that one should make sense of Mafia killings not by the test of whether they increase Mafia profits overall or achieve some other and more universal external end but by whether they suit the sum of Mafia life. But Mafia life is not self-contained and even those inescapably subject to it can surely ask why they should accept it. Making sense of cannibalism relative to the sum of the practices which constitute the life of cannibals is one thing; abandoning all further judgement another.

Questions about the rationality of rules are like those about preferences. They can be blocked for some purposes by retorting that, although there are sensible internal queries to raise about consistency of meaning or transitivity, in the end practices or preferences are 'given'. But, since one patently can ask whether misers have a rational preference for money over what it buys, or whether it is rational to live by one's code of honour, any ultimate block depends on dissolving the questions. For instance, one could try dissolving universal functionalist questions about how well different societies work on the grounds that societies are cultures, not mechanical systems. One could argue that questions about why people should accept their lot are out, because people, including ourselves, are not blind and mechanical rule-followers, cultural dopes or dupes, driven, rather than guided, by institutional structures of meaning. Yet to dissolve some kinds of question is not to dispose of all and we can still ask whether rules are finally their own warrant or can fail an enduring test of their rationality.

Wittgenstein may be finally ambiguous about where the questioning stops but he shows no sign of wanting to write social actors out of the human story. He insists that scrutiny of the rules alone will not let us decipher social action. Rule books are always incomplete, because what a rule is depends on how it is interpreted. There is always latitude in interpretation and, in interpreting, those who follow a rule also fill it in. They do so only partly, however, since the next new situation will call for further interpretation. Hence, in playing the game, we also help to construct it; and there can be no case for an analysis of rule-following which lets the game absorb the players and reduce them to ciphers.

Meanwhile, here is a lowlier reason to distance the players from the game. There is a difference between following rules and subscribing to them. For instance, a democratic party whose real aims would be unwelcome to most voters may try to win power by professing policies which are more broadly acceptable; and, within the party, a group seeking power is often similarly devious. So, indeed, is a single individual seeking power within a group seeking power. Given that policies and proposals can usually be presented in several ways, such tactics may or may not be dishonest; but the fact that they are common shows that the playing of games and roles with distance is entirely possible. Hence we should not confuse understanding what an action means overtly or what warrants it in its overt context with what actors are really up to in performing an action and what their own reasons or motives truly are. This is not to say that we are asocial selves, distanced from all our roles in all the games we play. For, as noted earlier, even if we need never be committed to the overt game of the moment, we may still necessarily be players in some game. (When a university honours some unadmirable but wealthy Croesus for the sake of benefactions to come, those who utter the sycophantic citations are presumably loyal servants of the university's covert purposes.) But, on the other hand, it does not settle the question of whether we are distinct from all our roles either.

We are thus embedded but not lost in the games of social life. Embeddedness may seem to make light of the problem of trust, since rules are normative and give rise to normative expectations which players of the game of course live up to. But, even on this sort of account, the distance granted to the players by making them interpreters of the rules keeps the problem alive. Meanwhile, if rationality is internalised and made a matter of doing what is locally appropriate, we seem to be offered a blanket endorsement of all practices which secure trust among participants; and no Enlightened thinker can settle for that. So can we accept that some social relations are integral to who we are and yet leave elbow room for critics of practices which secure trust? Where shall we dig in to prevent making a genuine virtue of whatever is deemed a virtue somewhere or other? To point the question, here are some further thoughts about honour.

Honour codes vary in how widely and deeply they apply. For example, in many American universities, they govern cheating in coursework and examinations but not the general conduct of life at large. Among the Mafia, they govern some relationships to an extent which conflicts with the rules of the wider society but, again, do not cover the whole of life. In other places and times, as perhaps with the Bushido code, they embody the defining framework of all conduct. Whatever their scope, however, they constitute types of action as honourable or dishonourable and regulate transactions and relationships accordingly. People bound by them are supplied with reasons of honour and given a way to decide what honour requires in new situations. These reasons are not of an instrumental, means-to-an-end sort, partly because the end is internal to the meaning conferred on action by the constitutive rules and partly because the manner of action counts for at least as much as its outcome. Persons of honour identify the honourable thing to do by applying the concepts of the code and then do it because it is the honourable thing.

The demands of honour are thus internally categorical and apply to situations which would not arise in their absence. For instance, what to do about an insult would not be a problem, unless the code defined the offending gesture or utterance as an insult. To outsiders, aware how codes vary, this gives honour a self-referential and relative character, which might even be quaint if it were not often a matter of life and death. For insiders, the demands are indeed categorical, even if they apply only to insiders. Nor are they less categorical for distinguishing between outsiders and insiders in some local, often graduated, way. Military honour, for example, tends to divide enemies into those to be respected, those to be treated as vermin and, in between, others to be viewed with a blend of respect and contempt which varies with their nationality or race. It also tends to classify non-combatants. For example, British officers in India in the heyday of the Raj were required to defend the honour of 'their' women but could treat inferior or outsider women much as they pleased; and their treatment of Indian women was often utterly dishonourable by the standards of other codes.

The example underlines the point that the demands of codes defining proper conduct for particular groups of people are not universal or uniform and are likely to conflict with Enlightenment ideas of morality. The sort of authority which tells people who they are, where they belong and how they should live needs only local standing; and many variants are viable. That is unsurprising, given the way in which honour codes tend to reinforce a distribution of power by issuing demands which recognise and endorse it. Honour among gentlemen is functional in a society which does not believe in equality for women.

Honour codes make people trustworthy, in the sense of reliable in keeping promises, or at least promises made to insiders. They so define and engage people's identities that having given one's word is a decisive reason for keeping it. But they do not thereby make people trustworthy, in the sense of deserving to be trusted. Fanatical racists, for instance, do not merit the trust which their bigotry makes possible. Nor is the success of honour among thieves a good reason for becoming a thief. So, although an internal, rule-related account of what gives action its meaning and makes it rational renders the problem of trust simple in some cases, it is not an account which suits trust-within-reason. On the contrary, where trust depends on defining the self with the aid of a distinction between insiders and outsiders, reason not only objects in theory but also, with the spread of Enlightenment, subverts it in practice.

Conclusion

This is no doubt a right and proper result of giving the problem an Enlightenment setting. But it should also make us uneasy. The original question was not why people do trust one another but whether and why it is rational for them to do so. The actual basis of trust is not simply irrelevant to it and anyone in the Enlightenment tradition would be disconcerted to find that trust is possible only in so far as people are not fully rational. Admittedly this is not what follows from the observation that some people are 'animals capable of promising' precisely because they are embedded in a form of life which prescribes the keeping of promises on pain of forfeiting one's self-respect. But recall how we came to explore the thought that trust has local origins. We set off up the Enlightenment Trail guided by reason, defined as instrumental rationality in the service of socially atomic individuals. Finding progress beyond The Rational Choice theoretically impossible, we switched reason to a universal, impartial and impersonal point of view. When this seemed too high-minded to yield the conditional nature of everyday trust, we next tried a less atomic, more socially embedded self. If that is illuminating, but only provided that rationality is internalised to particular rules for practical reasoning within a form of life, we should indeed be uneasy.

The uneasiness is in part to do with breaking the chain between truth, virtue and happiness. To preserve these links requires a universal standpoint from which to discriminate between different ways of embedding the self in social relations. Admittedly, the chain is already broken, unless reason extends to truth about values, but I refused to concede such a fact/value distinction earlier and it is not implied by the idea that the self is embedded in social relations. Nor, in a different context, need liberals refuse to sup with communitarians for fear of having to agree that all viable communities or traditions are equally satisfactory, although, no doubt, they would be wise to use a long spoon.

At any rate, we can persevere in refusing to let the self be absorbed and lost in the rules it follows, the games it plays, the roles it performs or the parts it acts out. In all these activities it is active in interpreting and active collectively in constructing the social fabric. That also makes it vital to keep a space for questioning institutions at large. Were this not rationally possible, much personal angst would be merely futile and philosophers and others who plumb the depths of ethics would be sadly misguided. The fact that people try to answer questions like 'How should one live?' or 'What is justice?' is not itself proof that a fully distanced point of view – a view from nowhere – is attainable, I admit. But faith in the attempt and the belief that it is possible are themselves some sign that we can conceive of ourselves in this way. Are there external as well as internal moral reasons? 'What has to be accepted, the given, is, so to say, *forms of life*' would deny it, if it were a remark about the relativity of cultural forms, and it is still a denial when 'forms of life' are construed in an external but non-moral way. But nothing in the present chapter requires being brow-beaten by *obiter dicta* which leave it mysterious how animals capable of promising are also capable of moral criticism.

A greater uneasiness is due to a dilemma about the personal and the impersonal. Trust, it seems, has to do with the former and reason with the latter. Liberal and communitarian thinking remain fundamentally different; and trust still eludes the former.

7
The bond of society

The crux remains how Adam can resist the lure of The Extra Trick and how both Hume's farmers are to get their harvests in. The problem arose initially because prudence addressed Adam in a language of forward-looking reasons, concerned solely with what would secure better consequences for him, as measured by his preferences over the possible outcomes. It advised him to take The Extra Trick if given the chance. But it also advised the equally rational Eve not to give him the chance, whether or not they had made an agreement; and, since both knew it, the trail ended sadly at The Rational Choice. Similarly, prudence told the second farmer to defect and told the first farmer to expect a defection. So they both lost their harvests 'for want of mutual confidence and security'. Trust had become rationally impossible. The point could be blunted by embodying a one-shot game in a series or by letting third parties know how these players had behaved for future reference. But it could not be so thoroughly overcome that cooperation became the basic form of social action, while prudence remained the governing idea. So, if prudence, speaking a language of homogenised utility and forward-looking reasons, is the voice of reason itself, then there is no trust within reason and critics will be right to say that the progress of Enlightenment destroys the bond of society.

Since then, we have tried complicating the character of a rational agent so that prudence can recommend indirect strategies. But neither a two-tiered preference structure nor a disposition to play fair with those who play fair could overcome the lure of a better bargain. We have also tried letting rational agents consider their situation impartially, finally by turning them into full-blooded Kantians. But, even with some nuancing of maxims, this had them behaving too unconditionally for a world where trust depends on experience and, even if somehow moralised, relates to how other people view a collective undertaking for what may or may not be a moral purpose. So, doubting whether full-blooded Kantians are suitably social, we tried embedding our rational agents in a form of life which supplied them with local reasons for, for instance, honourable conduct. But, although making trust possible, this put the source of obligation beyond reason and vulnerable to the spread of reason, a conscious and proper target for Enlightenment liberalism.

Yet, like Hume, I still hope for a remedy in the judgement and understanding for what is irregular and incommodious in the affections. The chapter will try to find one by getting rational agents to think in terms of joint enterprises. This is no minor amendment. It means equipping them to act as *reasonable* persons, essentially, if incompletely, social, who solve the problem of trust through socially mediated ties involving a generalised reciprocity. Elements of all the earlier attempts will be involved in the shift from 'rational' to 'reasonable'. Reasonable persons are not confined to forward-looking reasons and have a moral psychology which distances them from their preferences. They act on maxims suited to joint undertakings.

They also know who they are and where they belong. This will remain a vexed element. For instance, ties of family, friendship, honour, community or nationhood often provide not only place but also, somehow, identity. Tribes, communes and religious states often secure the loyalty of their members to one another. Reason endorses some such examples but not all. It needs to discriminate with a steady hand if reasonable persons are to differ from rational individuals without acquiring a wholly local identity and source of reasons for action. Conceptually, personal and social identity must be so related as to make it clear whether to accept or deny Rawls' remark that 'the self is prior to the ends which are affirmed by it'.[1] Politically, since the Enlightenment project is a dangerous failure unless it endorses some bonds of trust between socially located persons, we shall need to make sense of the delicate idea of a liberal community.

Historically, the Enlightenment Trail continues from Kant to Hegel and Marx, and then takes a contested route through later arguments about the state, the self and the citizen. At the end of the twentieth century its course is hard to discern. I could have charted how I think it goes by plotting other hostelries where tankards foam and ideas flow, starting with The Owl of Minerva, which opens only at dusk, and The Workers' Arms, where patrons can hunt and fish by day and spend their evenings talking philosophy in the back bar. But, being an analytical philosopher, I believe that the key options are those available by the end of the eighteenth century, at least if we are clear what to say about Rousseau. This chapter will see what can be done without him and the next will try factoring in his idea of 'a remarkable change in man'.[2]

PROBLEMS OF COORDINATION

The Enlightenment Trail sets the problem of trust both as a precise puzzle about rational strategic choice and as a grand enigma about the bond of a well-ordered society. I shall next pursue the precise puzzle, starting with the role of conventions in securing coordination and ending with some conclusions about the character of teamwork.

Although chapter 4 did not tackle the point, even coordination is

1. *A Theory of Justice*, p. 560.
2. *The Social Contract* (1762), book 1, chapter 8, in *Collected Writings of Rousseau, Volume 4*, ed. Roger D. Masters and Christopher Kelly, Dartmouth, N.H.: University Press of New England, 1994.

mysterious if we take a monocular view of joint action.[3] Assume that, as they head towards one another on the highway, Adam and Eve simply want to avoid a collision. Suppose that this requires only that they both keep left or both keep right and that there is a convention specifying 'Keep left' in the country where they live. So each keeps left – how could there be a puzzle about that?

All seems transparently simple, if we take the view of convention codified by David Lewis.[4] On his account, a convention is a regularity of which it is true, and recognised to be true, that almost everyone conforms, expects almost everyone to conform, prefers the results of general conformity to those of partial conformity, and would be as content with a different convention if almost all were similarly to adopt it. The idea can be illustrated by a two-person coordination game with two equilibria, like 'Coordination I' (below). Neither equilibrium is indicated in advance but, as soon as one becomes the regular choice, it can be relied on to continue. Suppose that 'left' emerges. Then Adam continues to keep left because he expects Eve to expect him to keep left. She, correspondingly, keeps left because she expects him to expect her to keep left. The convention is self-reinforcing and prudence can nod off in the knowledge that neither player has any reason to depart from it.

| | | *Eve* | |
		Right	Left
	Right	1, 1	0, 0
Adam			
	Left	0, 0	1, 1

Coordination I

3. What follows is much indebted to Robert Sugden in person and through his published work, for instance his paper 'Rational coordination' in F. Farina, F. Hahn and S. Vannucci (eds.), *Ethics, Rationality and Economic Behaviour*, Oxford: Clarendon Press, 1996, pp. 244–62. I am drawing too on our joint article 'Rationality in action'. Margaret Gilbert's *On Social Facts*, London: Routledge, 1989, is also very relevant.

4. D. K. Lewis, *Convention: A Philosophical Study*. Cambridge, Mass.: Harvard University Press 1969. My next sentence conveys the nub of his final definition of convention, given on p. 78.

When we analyse more carefully, however, we find a sleight of hand (apart from an ambiguity about the sense of 'expect', which will also concern us). The premises were hypothetical: 'Keep left *if* you expect the other to keep left.' The conclusion is categorical: '*Keep left!*' How did the hypothetical vanish? Well, it didn't. It would have done if either Adam or Eve were finally not making a strategic choice but, instead, were keeping left out of blind habit or after drawing a merely inductive conclusion from the regularities observed. In that case the choice of side would finally be a parametric one, with the parameters supplied by an independent element. Parametric choices need not reckon with the thought that my choice depends on yours and yours on mine. They do not involve a condition that *each* player keeps left *because* that is what the other expects. This condition, which is involved in Lewis' definition of convention, faces each strategic player among strategic players with a regress. Adam can expect Eve to expect him to keep left only if he expects her to expect him to expect her to expect him to keep left. . .; and so on. Once the regress starts, it continues to infinity, as befits the solipsistic situation of windowless monads whose point of view is recursively embedded, each within the other's.

The sleight of hand which telescopes the regress is tempting because the regress looks harmless: further extensions beyond the first step seem to add no further uncertainty. But it is still sleight of hand, since it involves something not included in the basic game-theory tool box. Before a convention emerges to solve the problem of coordination on the highway, prudence can say only 'Keep left if the other will keep left; and keep right if the other will keep right.' This is also all that it can say after the convention has emerged. Yet the convention itself is unconditional, saying flatly 'Keep left!' (in countries which keep left). The choices which contribute to its emergence cannot be solely strategic; nor can those which keep it going by relying on and thus reinforcing it. Provided that some drivers have a habit of keeping left or do so for reasons external to the coordination game, prudence can advise strategically minded other drivers to keep left too. But it has no unconditional advice on a highway used only by ideally rational drivers.

This may seem incredible. To make it more plausible, think of an election where *all* the voters are strategically minded and cannot decide whom to vote for without knowing how other voters intend to vote. Here it is plainer that reason cannot tell any voter unconditionally what to do. But, in practice, not all voters are strategically minded and so those who are can usually anchor their calculations. The highway is a purer case of coordination, where every way of succeeding is, in theory, equally satisfactory to all. Yet, if *all* players are rational agents, can they arrive at one in particular?

Thomas Schelling suggests an answer by appeal to 'focal points'.[5] In practice, he notes, one particular solution to a coordination problem often stands out in various ways. Thus, if Adam and Eve are shown an array of ten red and one blue objects and asked each to pick out one of them, with a reward for picking the same one, they will have no trouble in picking the blue one. If they are asked similarly to name a day of the year or a city in America, Adam will 'see' that Christmas day is a better day than his own birthday and Eve will 'see' that New York is a more promising city than one she happens to be fond of herself. This solution is not available to formalised game theory, which can only recommend random choices here, because it deals only in abstract choices between abstracted players.

Focal points take us part of the way. Adam picks not what is salient for himself (his birthday) but what he thinks will be salient for Eve, given that she is thinking along similar lines. Each thus converges on the same salient. But the psychological fact that they recognise salients and can realise that coordination requires a salient which both players recognise does not solve the puzzle in full. To make this plain, we can build an obvious salient into an abstract coordination game by making one way of coordinating superior. In 'Coordination II' (below) it is positively scandalous if X is not the uniquely rational strategic choice for each player. Yet prudence can still give each only hypothetical advice: 'Choose X if the other will choose X; choose Y if the other will choose

5. T. C. Schelling, *The Strategy of Conflict*. Cambridge, Mass.: Harvard University Press, 1960, *e.g.* pp. 297–8.

Y.' The moral is not that coordination is rationally impossible but that it requires an unconditional element so far mysterious.

	Eve	
	X	Y
X	2, 2	0, 0
Y	0, 0	1, 1

Eve (top header), *Adam* (left label)

Coordination II

The mystery is not the element itself, since Schelling's ideas about focal points are widely accepted, but how it works. Here Hume offers what are broadly still the leading answers. One is to invoke 'Custom or Habit', which he describes as 'the great guide of human life' and the foundation of all our reasonings.[6] But this cannot satisfy anyone trying to traverse the Enlightenment Trail by the pure light of reason and, in any case, it does not plug the hole. I do not mean that custom and habit are guides which it is always irrational to follow. Where life is short and calculation costly, reliance on them is entirely rational. The custom of putting a striped pole outside barbers' shops saves the time and trouble of trying to get one's hair cut at the butcher's, baker's or candlestick maker's. Habits too can be sensible. The rational way to drive a car is not to calculate every change of gear or speed but to become so used to driving that no conscious thought is needed. Habitual or customary behaviour and intelligent action often coalesce. But the suggestion that habit (psychological) or custom (social) can ground norms is another matter.

What makes it rational to adhere to custom or habit is not the mere fact that they are established. It is that they are helpful in the pursuit of ends not defined by custom or habit alone. This is plainer for habit. It is no excuse for causing an accident that one was not thinking. Drivers must remain alert for signs that habit is about to let them down. They

6. *Enquiry Concerning Human Understanding*, v. 1, 36.

do well to give reason a back seat but not to let it go to sleep. Yet that is a puzzling image. There are occasions when reason needs to be stood down completely. The tightrope walker, if consciously alert, may wobble. The skater on thin ice should throw caution to the winds. But this is not what makes sense for drivers, who need, so to speak, to stand reason half down and give it a watching brief. Is there a state between full control and watching helplessly as the unthinking driver overtakes a police car at 100 mph? Where habit is truly motivating, I do not see how there can be; and, where not, we are no further forward.

Custom introduces a new line of thought. Hume tends to treat it as synonymous with habit. But, whereas habit threatens to empty action of its meaning, custom is often a source of meaning. The rational way to dress for a Western funeral, for example, is in sober garments. This is not because it saves time deciding what to wear, or even simply because that is the Western way (in contrast to cultures where something colourful is expected). We dress symbolically for funerals, as part of an occasion meant to celebrate a life and mourn a death. The meaning bears on what we might say about whether dressing according to custom is rational, irrational or non-rational. It is not exactly an instrumentally rational action, because means do not stand to ends in the performance of ceremonies as they do in opening a can of sardines. Wearing black may be an effective symbol but it is not exactly an efficient means to an end. Yet what defines proper conduct at funerals and the reasons for it is not so wholly internal to the customary practice to which funerals belong that it ceases to be instrumental at all. The rituals make sense only if (some of) those present believe that a properly conducted occasion achieves an external end. Hence habit, being psychological, suits a desire/belief model of action better than custom, which involves social meanings. But neither makes it rational to follow norms for a reason external to them which is binding and overrides reasons to renege.

Hume's other answer is, as we saw earlier, that 'nature provides a remedy, in the judgement and understanding, for what is irregular and incommodious in the affections'. What is incommodious is our partiality towards ourselves, and the remedy is to adopt an impartial standpoint. This line is more appealing to anyone trying to find the basis of trust-within-reason. But it does not explain why it is rational to coordinate on the uniquely best equilibrium in 'Coordination II'. The idea is that Adam and Eve will each do well to follow some general rule or principle addressed to everyone in their position: here, for instance, that they should choose the strategy which contributes to an outcome uniquely preferred by all. Call this (or some more general version) 'the principle of coordination'. It is clearly a splendid principle and, if followed by all, will solve the problem. But there's the rub. For all to follow it, each must do so; and it remains rational for each only if others will. Even if XX is worth more to each than YY, the principle does not cancel the advice 'Choose Y if other(s) choose Y', and so is merely *ad hoc* unless it operates at a deeper level than is yet on offer.

So how do we shed the conditional element introduced by making the players ideally rational? The two answers most attractive are for Adam and Eve each to shift from an individual to a universal point of view, and for them to play as a team. But both require amending the initial individualism in ways which we are now ready to explore.

Liberals may prefer to try a universal point of view, since that seems less of a threat to individualism. It simply requires philosophical egoists to switch to judging outcomes not by the pay-off to self but by some other criterion. The obvious one is the total (or average) pay-off, with the result that rational individuals become utilitarians in the moral philosophers' sense. This is a temporary and limited conversion, presumably, for occasions which are more typically a matter of whether to keep right or left on the highway here and now than of how to coordinate the future of the human race. Even so it runs into some snags of a wider utilitarianism. This becomes clear if we return to the harvest problem and suggest that the farmers should each aim for the maximum total utility, thus requiring A to help with B's harvest. That sounds a good idea until we notice that, although the total utility in the original setting was greater if B helped A in return ((1,1), as compared with (-1,2)), this need not have been so. The version below, 'Harvesting with New Figures', has the same crux but the total is greater if B takes advantage of A. Here, as even a temporary and limited utilitarian, A should still do his bit, it seems, and positively prefer that B then plays down (a net total of 3 utils) rather than across (thus securing both harvests).

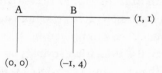

Harvesting with New Figures

Those who dislike the look of this can temporise in various ways. They might try objecting to the interpersonal comparison of utilities. That would open a discussion of whether welfare economics and the theory of social choice can and should be conducted without calibrating the utility scales of different individuals. But I have never understood how one can be a utilitarian in moral philosophy or social policy, unless willing and able to compare different people's pay-offs when choosing between welfare programmes. It has to make sense to compare distributions like $(1,1)$, $(-1,2)$ and $(-1,4)$ and suggest that the first or last two are decisively different from a universal point of view. In that case, however, one cannot object that A will not cooperate next year if done down now. Anyone wholly serious about total (or average) utilities has to deem it rational for A to accept being done down every year, if it were true in every year that B was made happier by playing down than A was made miserable.

A more direct retort is that playing utilitarian in a coordination game does not commit A and B to doing the same in all games. But why not? A ready answer is that it is rational for A, who was only pretending to be a utilitarian for the sake of getting the benefits of coordination, to revert when the pretence does not pay. In that case, however, we are still dealing with philosophical egoists and the shift, being merely a tactical device, is not a genuine shift to the universal. Hence it does not help with coordination either, since we are back with conditional advice: 'Play utilitarian *if* the other player does likewise.'

So a reply is called for which pays more than lip-service to a universal standpoint. In a broader context, this might be a cue for utilitarians to reassure individualists by introducing indirect devices, like entrenching liberties and individual rights, and perhaps by replacing Act-utilitarianism with Rule- or Motive-utilitarianism. But the resulting discussion of when a utilitarian stops being a utilitarian would take us too far afield. Instead, we can try setting a lower limit, so that A simply refuses to play the utilitarian strategy in any game where it leaves him worse off than he would be by not taking part at all. He can hardly be expected to take part in a cooperation designed to gain the benefits of cooperation if there will be no benefits for him! Yet, when he plays, he plays as a genuine utilitarian.

But can he be a genuine enough utilitarian on these terms? Genuine utilitarians act on principle and accede to the best distribution of the highest total, even if it is not best for them in particular. Can tacticians be relied on not to opt out when it suits? The injection of enough individualism to ensure that no one is made worse off by taking part in the game does not meet the point. This is an impersonal, liberal restriction on a universal standpoint which, in itself, can have illiberal implications, since universalists acting on behalf of God or the state may have no inhibitions about sacrificing individuals. Tactical subscribers to the restriction remain interested in whether they could do better for themselves in particular. Genuine subscribers have a principled position which removes this bias to oneself without granting that all universalist solutions are equally good.

A principled way of confining solutions to those which benefit both players casts a wider net even for coordination. Suppose that the outcome better for both A and B has bad consequences for third parties. For example, coordinating on a low price for copper may make A and B rich, but at the expense of small firms who supply it or of developing countries where it is mined. Such externalities can certainly be included, for instance through a Lockean proviso to prevent injury to third parties, and this would be in keeping with an Enlightenment project linking truth, virtue and happiness worldwide. But what began as a narrow question of what makes it rational for A and B each to aim at a Pareto-superior salient then ramifies into full-blown moral questions about the good of humanity at large. That may sound like a mistake, on the grounds that a universal point of view which lets A and B coordinate cannot truly involve considering more people than A and B. But why not? Otherwise the universal standpoint will remain subordinate to their separate individual aims, and so, whatever its wider bearing, is still to be acted on by each only if the other does too. Hence universalism, with or without a liberal restriction, solves the problem only if it is adopted wholeheartedly.

TRUST IN MINIATURE: TEAMWORK

In that case, at least for anyone wishing to steer clear of ethics, the other solution is better focused: A and B coordinate by playing as a team. The idea seems innocent of moral considerations, both internal and external. How teams distribute benefits and burdens among their members depends simply on the purpose of forming the team and does not raise questions about the good of humanity at large. Teams tend to distinguish insiders ('our side') from outsiders ('the other lot'), thus making something special of membership. Since teams often compete for positional goods like power and glory, the success of winners can be bad news for losers. But, since not every division of people into 'them' and 'us' is objectionable, we can discuss teams before thinking about ethics.

How exactly does a team solution work? Formally, it replaces conditional advice with unconditional demands. Adam can decide what to do by reflecting that the good of the team requires Adam to do *a* and Eve to do *e*, and then treat this as an unconditional reason to do his bit. It no longer worries him that he does well to do *a* only if Eve will indeed do *e*, because Eve will have a similarly unconditional reason for doing *e* as her bit. Each now has the assurance that the other will not wait to contribute. (The other may, of course, fail through incompetence or bad luck; but this will already have been allowed for in working out the best strategy for the team and hence for each player.) If their team does best by having both keep left, then each keeps left without further ado.

This is not simply an assurance game with the assurance duly supplied. To prevent conditionals from resurfacing, team membership needs to be a stronger relation than membership of a mere association. One way to make the point is to say that members of teams have '*we*-intentions': each, if asked 'What do you intend to do?', replies '*We* intend to keep left.' This will be no small innovation, if *we*-intentions presuppose *we*-desires and *we*-beliefs, in short if teams or groups can be agents only if they have the relevant attributes of individual agents. But that is not a *nolle prosequi* and persuasive attempts have been made to work out the analytical apparatus needed for group-agency.[7] Taking this as read, the question becomes how robust a sense to give to the reality of teams, as distinct from that of mere associations.

There are, I think, two robust ways of conceiving of teams and hence of actions done for the good of a team. One is to think of the team as an entity transcending its members, with a good which transcends and determines theirs. The other is to think of team membership as a constitutive relation between what are still separate people. Christian marriage, for instance, can be conceived in either way. It might be a union so complete that Adam and Eve become, as the Bible puts it, one flesh – a single new person distinct from each of them. Or marriage might be a partnership short of a merger, with Adam and Eve deeply but not exclusively committed to doing what is collectively best for two partners. Both ideas of marriage differ from the one suited to Las Vegas weddings and Mexican divorces, that marriage is an association for purposes of mutual back-scratching. But this example is merely illustrative and, rather than taking it further or trying others like the Trinity as one person and three or the Church as a single body instanced in many places and times, I adjourn discussion until we have cleared a space for Rousseau to take it further.

A way of thinking about teams which removes the conditional

---

7. For example, John Searle espouses *we*-intentions in *The Construction of Social Reality*, Harmondsworth: Allen Lane, The Penguin Press, 1995, pp. 24–7, where he claims that 'collective intentionality is a biologically primitive phenomenon'. For thorough attempts to work out what is involved, see Gilbert, *On Social Facts*, and Raimo Tuomela, *The Importance of Us*, Stanford University Press, 1995.

element in coordination also bears on the harvest problem, where a team-solution for the farmers would have ramifying implications. Since they face a Prisoner's Dilemma (in an extended form, where the second player will know what the first has chosen), a solution would apply to the standard one-shot game. Since what they face is also a two-legged centipede (so to speak), there would be implications for longer centipedes, like the Enlightenment Trail and repeated Prisoner's Dilemmas, and for the riddle of backward induction in general. Admittedly, the difference remains that the farmers need to play out of equilibrium in a way vulnerable to bargain-hunting, whereas coordinators are in search of an equilibrium. But the connecting thought is that teams have a common good to which it is rational for members to contribute, provided that membership is a robust enough relation to secure decision-making at this level. The question is whether teams can be primary in the sense required.

Rational choice theorists should now be in two minds. On the one hand, the connections cannot be made within even an expanded game theory, while the basic logic of choice still bids the second farmer defect, if the game were to get so far, and bids each player in a one-shot Prisoner's Dilemma choose an equilibrium strategy which sums to mutual defection. That suggests denying the reality of the new level. On the other hand, rational choice theory is supposed to show why the best choices are best; and it is hard to deny that farmers whose team-work has produced an abundance have chosen rationally. What holds for the harvest goes for plenty of other occasions too, for example the coin game in chapter 3, where the opening player takes two and kills the game, however many million are on the table. On balance, then, it looks as if the new level should be accepted, since the riddle of backward induction is a scandal for game theory, rather than a sad fact of life among (rational) persons.

It may still be that backward induction can be given a technical fix, for instance by suggesting that any shadow of uncertainty about what a player will do has a multiplier effect. But, for the purpose in hand, I continue to assume that the problem lies deeper than technicalities, because uncertainty so breeds uncertainty that a paradox emerges. Let

Adam, being a rational agent in the standard sense, contemplate a cooperative move. To decide whether to pass the first pub, he must estimate how likely Eve would then be to pass the second. She would have to judge how likely it is that Adam is a rational agent. If she decides that he probably is not, she will continue the walk, in which case Adam would have made a rational decision and Eve would have miscalculated. So she should have decided to halt. But, in that case, he would not have made a rational choice and her previous reasoning stands. So she should continue; and so on. Paradox breeds paradox and the theory implodes.

Barring a technical fix, I conclude that truly rational agents are not finally confined to forward-looking reasons. It cannot be true that bygones are always bygones, implying that each choice is as if the start of a new game. The fact that one harvest has been gathered, that half the coins have been successfully collected or that Adam and Eve are further along the trail than The Rational Choice has to be construable as a reason for continuing. This calls for an animal truly capable of promising and hence for an amendment to the abstraction which reduced all motivation to its representation by forward-looking expected utility numbers.

The question is then whether rational choice theory can find room for agents motivated by team spirit. In so far as the theory abstracts from social life, it is worth reflecting that everyday encounters involve ambiguity. Even friends (or enemies) cannot always be totally sure of one another's reasons, and relative strangers may often need to hesitate. Although simple coordination is a team-game free of temptation to exploit the team, it is not always plain in practice that all players are seeking simply to coordinate. Hence everyday strategic choice needs more information than can be represented by figures in a matrix. Whereas game theory treats all matrices with Prisoner's Dilemma pay-offs as Prisoner's Dilemmas, we might suggest that 'reasonable' persons discriminate by whether the other player is a friend, enemy or stranger and according to the character and context of the encounter. The question for rational choice theory is whether such ambiguities can only be treated as uncertainties about true pay-offs and probabilities, as distinct from recognising that people often but not always play as teams.

If the ambiguity can be recognised, it will be pervasive. Eyeing a centipede, Adam and Eve may each intend to do what serves them best as a team if given reason to expect the other to do likewise. The fact of having managed the first leg might be such a reason. But, with two kinds of motivation possible, it is also consistent with a malign attempt to induce the other player to believe that team spirit is operating. Hence players can no longer be as transparent to each other as assumed when postulating Common Knowledge of Rationality. That has large implications for the use of the usual ideal-type theorising.

Yet, the Common Knowledge assumption always was a curious abstraction from a social world where Adam and Eve, being distinct persons, are necessarily somewhat opaque to one another. People who know one another well can become translucent but never wholly transparent. They can never be like two sub-routines of a single computer programme, for example black and white in a chess computer set to 'self-play' mode. By abstracting Adam and Eve from their normal and normative social relations, information which guides their everyday decisions is lost. It would be odd if the loss of information involved in turning neighbours into perfect strangers could be more than compensated by giving them common knowledge of rationality. Indeed, I find it unsurprising that perfect strangers cannot trust one another to play centipede games as neighbours would. So dropping the Common Knowledge assumption would be no sorrow, if the theory can survive it.

But can it? Being unclear how far the implications would reach, I shall answer the riddle of backward induction only tentatively. My tentative conclusion is that flesh-and-blood persons have reasons for action which are alien to their abstract counterparts. These reasons are not sentiments, which can be represented in utilities, but normative features of a situation which they have partly inherited and partly created. That is finally why the joint agency, which would solve their problem, cannot be introduced into the theory of games without upheaval. Hence the standard theory is only provisional. It applies in full wherever pay-offs in goods can be represented in utils; and much can be understood about social interaction through this style of analysis. But, since it cannot dispel the paradoxes with only its own resources, it is not a general theory of practical reason. Economics, one might say, is finally no more a self-contained discipline than the economy is an isolable realm of social life.[8]

Conclusion

The chapter is titled 'The bond of society' and one might have hoped that an appeal to the virtues of game theory would account for the bond itself. But the conclusion is at best that game theory shows just what is needed and at worst that it simply relies on an idea beyond its scope. Yet the idea itself is now clear, even if its secret is not. The farmers get both their harvests in if they can trust one another to play as a team. Does success mean that the farmers have chosen rationally or that the team has? That is the crux. The answer which tempts me is that we can regard the team as shorthand for the farmers, provided that the relationship between them involves a suitable kind of reciprocity. This is a reciprocity which cannot be expressed solely in forward-looking reasons for action, as I shall next try to show. We thus embark on what I earlier called the grand enigma of trust, still in search of social relations which reason can endorse.

8. This line of thought is fleshed out in Martin Hollis, 'Moves and motives', *Analysis*, 50 (1990), pp. 49–62, reprinted in *Reason in Action*, pp. 62–79.

8
Trust in the light of reason

Progress along the Enlightenment Trail depends on relating Adam and Eve in a way which satisfies the demands of teamwork and which liberals can accept. Since these conditions still threaten to conflict, the trail remains difficult. I shall open the final attempt by thinking about reciprocity and a contrast begun in chapter 6. One idea of it is initially bilateral and, although extendable to a wider circle, retains the idea that debts and obligations must be to the overall benefit of the persons acquiring them. The other is a generalised reciprocity, whose form is that, because A has hurt or helped B, C owes something to D. The conflict springs from trying to read this both universally and locally. Either way corrects the bilateral version but one requires the self to be abstracted and the other embedded. This emerges when the motives of blood donors are considered with the aid of John Rawls' idea of reciprocity, and will lead us to another such idea, one which involves what Rousseau termed 'a remarkable change in man'. The aim is to make sense of a final hope that citizens in a local community can also be citizens of the world. To achieve it, we must also challenge Condorcet's typical Enlightenment notion of the political and moral sciences, however, before we can hope for a positively free world order. That

gives liberals much to fight over as well as for, and the book ends spec-
ulatively in recommending trust in the light of reason.

RECIPROCITY

Among mutual back-scratchers, reciprocity is at heart bilateral:
you scratch my back and I scratch yours; if you scratched mine yesterday, I owe you one today. But the circle can be expanded, so that I can
pay my debt by scratching the back of someone who scratches yours,
or someone who scratches someone's who scratches yours. As this
ramifies, we can form a backscratchers' association, where scratching
any back gains a credit, cashed in by having one's back scratched by
anyone wanting a credit in their turn. Baby-sitting rings often work in
this way, with a system of vouchers so that all parents sit and are sat for
without its needing to be true that, if A has sat for B, then B will have sat
for A. (Interestingly, such rings often insist on payment in kind, not
cash, so that all parents shall do their bit in person.) Reciprocity, which
starts as bilateral, can thus be generalised.

A baby-sitting ring is geared to consequentialist reasons connected
with mutual benefits. But, even if some examples of generalised reciprocity are of this amiable and finally forward-looking sort, others are
not. Two kinds of reciprocity are involved and not only the nice and
nasty varieties of one. Think, for instance, of the feud between the
houses of Capulet and Montague, which forms the backdrop to *Romeo
and Juliet* and runs through the story from the opening duel between
Tybalt and Mercutio to the final deaths of Romeo and Juliet themselves. None of these characters was party to whatever sparked the
feud, but all are caught without escape. A vendetta which obliges the
kin of one party to kill the kin of the other provides reasons which
make sense only in terms of past actions coupled with the fittingness
of revenge. This is generalised reciprocity involving non-consequen-
tial reasons for doing what, here, is not to mutual advantage.

Generalised reciprocity can thus have a dark side. But it need not;
and, either way, it is not always a matter of mutual advantage. Why, for
instance, do drivers pick up hitch-hikers? Given risks which range from
boring conversation to physical violence, it can seem a puzzling prac-

tice. But then, even if some drivers are simply full of the milk of human kindness, others have reasons of a different construction. For myself, I recall younger days without a car and give lifts out of generalised gratitude for the lifts then received. Also I tend to stop for people who look like students. This is because my student sons have travelled far in the cars of amiable strangers and I feel a blend of vicarious gratitude and mild obligation to reciprocate. If asked whether this gives me a good reason, I hesitate. I have the good Humean reason that my sympathy is prompted by an image of my sons standing on rainswept kerbs waving hopeful thumbs. But that is not to do with reciprocity. Is the fact that other drivers have helped my sons in the past a good reason for me to help other students now? If good reasons had to be forward-looking, the answer would plainly be no. But, even granted other sorts of reasons for action, an inference from 'Someone unknown to me helped someone else last year' to 'I should help someone now' still looks flimsy, even if I add that the person helped last year is my son. Yet there is no doubting that such motives operate or that such practices are common, whether or not we can finally regard them as rational.

Thus prompted, consider the deeper example of blood-donors. In Britain blood for transfusions is collected from volunteers, who receive no visible return beyond a cup of weak tea while they recuperate. Why do they do it? When Richard Titmuss conducted a survey of donors in the 1960s, he found the commonest reply to be 'I might need blood myself one day.'[1] Intriguingly, this response makes no rational 'economic' sense. The blood I give today will not be restored to me if I need some next year, nor does my giving it make it significantly likelier that there will be enough blood for me then. My gift puts me no higher in the queue if supplies are short. Admittedly, even a tiny contribution does something to keep the practice of blood-giving alive and well, rather as individual votes in a democracy, however instrumentally futile when considered individually, sum to a flourishing democracy. But that does not meet the point that the national blood bank, like a

1. R. M. Titmuss, *The Gift Relationship: From Human Blood to Social Policy*, London: Allen and Unwin, 1970.

healthy democracy, is a public good dependent on voluntary contributions. (What about Australia, where there is a small fine for not voting
and democracy is in good health? Even if the fine accounts for a high
turn-out, I still argue that so small a penalty activates the citizenly
motive, rather than replaces it.) By contrast, an instrumentally rational individual, directly weighing only costs and benefits to self, obeys
the dominant logic of the free-rider problem and chooses not to
contribute. Nor does it alter the balance, I reckon, to suggest that some
donors receive a warm glow of smug inner satisfaction along with
their cup of weak tea.

Hence, unless the respondents were simply stupid, the reply that 'I
might need blood myself one day' was a cover for a non-economic
motive which they did not care to voice. Or so the director of one
regional centre assured me, while endorsing Titmuss as still an accurate guide to today's pattern. Titmuss himself saw the National Blood
Transfusion Service as a system of gifts between strangers who claim
'no explicit or implicit right to a return gift or action' and are moved by
'creative altruism'. (Although no donors were 'purely altruistic' in the
sense of 'complete, disinterested spontaneous altruism', all evidenced
'some sense of obligation', even if 'perhaps encouraged by a vague
sense that the system might benefit them one day'.) Through creative
altruism 'the self is realised with the help of anonymous others' – a
vital component of a flourishing society, he maintained.

The underlying motive presumably surfaced in the next most
common replies: 'Other people are in need of blood' and 'Someone I
know would recently have died but for a blood transfusion.' Although
both can be converted into universal Kantian maxims, they can also be
read as having a more local import. The first may have only fellow citizens in mind or those within the ambit of the National Blood
Transfusion Service. The second generalises readily to the donor's
friends, relatives and neighbours but may stop there. Even if it goes
further, it still suggests generalised reciprocity, rather than universal
duty. This is not to dispute the element of creative altruism but to
temper it with a sense of contributing to particular networks which
command one's loyalty. That in turn is not inconsistent with a practical

awareness that such networks offer collective mutual support and insurance to their members. Blood donation sustains a public good for a particular community and the donors' 'vague sense that the system might benefit them one day' can put down a local marker without thereby showing them up as egoistic individuals after all.

Motives which are relatively selfless, being selfless relative to one's own community, and which have a by-product of realising the self, seem to me a possible gloss on 'man's asocial sociality'. We contribute because the Transfusion Service needs blood to pass on to those it serves. The shift from an individual to a relatively universal point of view depends on the relativity: it is *our* blood. This is, so to speak, philosophical egoism in the first person plural, where the *we* is neither a sum of associated individuals nor all of humanity but a matter of membership. Titmuss is right, I think, to call the practice one of 'gifts between strangers' but these are *relative* strangers – unknown members of *our* network.

This way of reading the score answers a question which has often puzzled me. Why do people who contribute to public goods fret about free-riders in some cases but not others? There is a logic of 'enough', I submit, which can overcome the dominance of defection, provided that a sense of membership is in play. Donors cooperate if confident that enough blood is being provided by enough members. Thus, public goods which depend on creative altruism are a matter both of a large enough total to secure the good and of enough contributors for mutual reassurance that contributing is a worthy activity. Enough is then enough. I do not say that all donors work like this. There may well be some altruists who give their blood regardless and would do so as readily if the scheme were world-wide. There may also be some psychological egoists seeking the social approval gained by a display of public spirit. I suggest only that there is a group of donors whose creative altruism is local and conditional, a matter of there being enough members for a joint undertaking. For persons who flourish in networks, generalised reciprocity is a rational expression of who they are and where they belong.

A reciprocity which goes with membership makes sense of the idea that C can have an obligation to help D for the reason that A has helped B. Such obligations are neither straightforwardly moral nor morally neutral. Also they can conflict, where people belong to several networks, thus raising a question of how to settle priorities. Friendship, freemasonry, patriotism and thieves' honour share a power to bind insiders *in foro interno*, which is part of what we are seeking. Reason does not endorse them indiscriminately, however, and we still need a criterion for deciding when to uphold a scheme of quasi-moral, social obligations and when to subvert it.

A more persuasive name for such a scheme is 'political', in keeping with Locke's remark that trust is the bond of society. Politics is a realm of obligations which are binding on dissenters in virtue of membership and are neither straightforwardly moral nor simply morally neutral. What is the political way to treat obligations which go with reciprocity?

It is instructive to see what John Rawls says about it in the context of 'a well-ordered society'. In both *A Theory of Justice* and *Political Liberalism*, he makes it clear that 'a fair system of cooperation between free and equal persons' involves reciprocity. In the earlier book, he introduces 'the idea of reciprocity implicit in the notion of a well-ordered society' as early as page 14. It thus attends both his initial suggestion that rational economic individuals, meeting behind a veil of ignorance, will form a just society as a matter of mutual advantage, and his broader line that we are 'reasonable persons' with enough of a natural sense of justice to solve the problem of trust. Yet, throughout *A Theory of Justice*, 'reciprocal' seems always to mean 'mutual' (as in 'reciprocal advantage'); and reciprocity is not of the fully generalised sort. Thus, section 75 presents three psychological laws about how children come to reciprocate love, friendly feeling and trust towards those who treat them with love and fairness: 'The basic idea is that of reciprocity, a tendency to answer in kind.' What is basic here is reciprocating towards one's own benefactors.

Political Liberalism introduces what purports to be a fully generalised reciprocity. In contrast to the earlier book, it grounds the fair system of cooperation in an overlapping historical consensus (and thus dispenses with any explicitly metaphysical notion of the self). The members of a well-ordered society are squarely 'reasonable persons', rather than rational economic individuals, the difference being connected with generalised reciprocity. Although reasonable persons are not moved by the general good as such, they 'desire for its own sake a social world in which they, as free and equal, can cooperate with others on terms all can accept. They insist that reciprocity should hold within that world so that each benefits along with the others' (p. 50). This echoes pp. 16–17, where 'the idea of reciprocity lies between the idea of impartiality, which is altruistic (being moved by the general good), and the idea of mutual advantage understood as everyone's being advantaged with respect to each person's present or future situation as things are'. The generalised character of this reciprocity is again stressed, when Rawls adds 'the further point that reciprocity is a relation between the citizens of a well-ordered society expressed by its public political conception of justice. Hence the two principles of justice... formulate an idea of reciprocity between citizens.'

These remarks set the problem which we have just reached, however. A reciprocal relation among citizens which lies between impartiality and mutual advantage has become fundamental to his whole account of a well-ordered society. Yet I have just cited (almost) all the references to reciprocity in both books and remain puzzled. If we take the general good, promoted by impartiality, to be what benefits everyone and suppose that 'reasonable persons' are rational individuals with a modicum of altruism, then nothing 'lies between' altruism and advantage. Altruism directs the benefits of reciprocity to whoever would benefit most, whereas mutual self-interest directs them to those party to an essentially commercial scheme. What 'lies between' would presumably be a distribution which recognises both general need and particular obligation. But, given Rawls' robust individualism, these claimants exert irreconcilable pressures, with altruism, despite Kantian overtones, bidding us act like utilitarians, and mutual self-interest, despite utilitarian overtones, bidding us confine ourselves to our own creditors. I do not see how a self conceived as 'prior to the ends which are affirmed by it' can cope. If so, it is

fair comment to call the scheme one which *purports* to be a fully generalised reciprocity.

'A REMARKABLE CHANGE IN MAN'

This is finally the cue for Rousseau, who has been waiting patiently
for the Enlightenment Trail to hit trouble caused by reliance on an
untrammelled individualism. I do not imply that Rousseau speaks for
the Enlightenment, since that is a vexed question and there is argument both ways even for texts which seem clearly on one side or the
other.[2] In *The Social Contract*, he seeks a form of association 'by means
of which each one, uniting with all, nevertheless obeys only himself
and remains as free as before' (book 1, chapter 6). He finds it in a society
of citizens, where everyone accepts the core obligation of membership, namely to submit to the General Will of the citizen-body and to
obey its rulings on all matters which it decides to rule on. This is an
alarmingly strong form of association, perhaps too strong for liberals.
Yet it falls short of merging individuals into a union where their individual identity is lost. They retain *amour de soi* and *amour propre*, despite
'a remarkable change in man' which transforms individuals into citizens. This is clear from Rousseau's elegant statement of the crux for
the Enlightenment Trail:

> each individual can, as a man, have a particular will contrary to or differing
> from the general will he has as a citizen. His particular interest can speak to
> him quite differently from the common interest. His absolute and naturally
> independent existence can bring him to view what he owes the common cause
> as a free contribution, the loss of which will harm others less than its payment
> burdens him.[3]

This sets a classic free-rider problem by making it rational for each
individual to shirk his contribution to a common good, even though it
is also his own good. Free-riding by all would lead to the ruin of the
body politic. The 'remarkable change' lets our interests as citizens

---

2. See, for instance, John Hope Mason's fine article 'Individuals in society: Rousseau's
   republican vision' in *History of Political Thought*, 10 (1989), pp. 89–112. I have gained
   much from talking to him.
3. *The Social Contract*, book 1, chapter 7.

prevail in public affairs, and lets our common interests prevail over our individual ones in personal matters. It is described in book I, chapter 8, where an individual in the state of nature is 'a narrow, stupid animal', moved by instinct – physical impulses and appetites which lead him to consider only himself; and a citizen is 'a creature of intelligence and a man', moved by justice – the voice of duty prompting him to consult reason in order to arrive at what is right. In sum, what he loses is his natural liberty to grab what he can; what he gains is civil liberty to enjoy what is legally his within the framework set by the General Will. With civil liberty, Rousseau adds, comes 'moral freedom', which 'makes a man master of himself' and is attached to the thought that 'the impulse of appetite alone is slavery, and obedience to the law one has prescribed for oneself is freedom'.

This sounds like Kantian universalism. But Rousseau has something more local and particular in mind. The General Will is that of a particular society, the will of a localised set of citizens. It can override a liberal distinction between what is right and what is good, which would confine the law-making to procedural rules of fair play and thus leave us free individually to pursue our own good in our own way. Where a General Will exists, it is entitled to rule on any matter whatever; and, if it does deem some matters private, it can always revoke this concession.[4] In short, Rousseau is not thinking in terms of individual rights or mutually convenient rules protecting private life and personal morality. He is out to forge a moral bond for an uncorrupt society. His 'moral freedom' is not the freedom to be moral after one's own fashion but must take the form of 'obedience to the law one has prescribed for oneself'. Although he adds stiff conditions which must be satisfied if a General Will is to emerge, different societies can presumably prescribe different views of how their citizens should live.

What this comes to depends on how one construes the interplay between citizens as separate persons and the common power with which they compel dissenters. Preferences are both consulted and

4. 'It is agreed that each person alienates through the social compact only that part of his power, goods and freedom whose use matters to the community; but it must also be agreed that the Sovereign alone is the judge of what matters' (book II, chapter 4).

constructed in the civic process. As citizens, we bring to collective decision-making the intimate aims, emotions and relations which make us particular human beings. Yet we stand ready to revise these identities if the General Will, as the outcome of the interplay, demands it. Although we are who we are, not what we want, we have a collective moral freedom to determine who we should be.

That creates a deep ambiguity which, if resolved squarely in favour of the collective and communal, leads directly to the totalitarian state which critics have often accused Rousseau of licensing. The crux lies in the priority between 'I' and 'we'. The self, taken individually, is not prior to the ends which are affirmed by it. But neither are those ends prior to what we affirm collectively. They are affirmed as a result of a civic process in which each of us takes part. But the authority of the process is Rousseau's answer to the question 'How can a man be forced to obey wills not his own?', thus threatening our individuality. Yet we each remain 'as free as before'. The individual self thus slips from view in the interplay of 'I' and 'we', but, Rousseau claims, retains the individuality of its particular interests when acquiring a civic identity and duties.

Does Rousseau leave us with a triumphant paradox or an intractable crux? I am never sure. He locates the key deep in personal life, in a dialectic of reason and feeling, or reason and nature, and offers a political resolution. In obeying the General Will 'each associate obeys only himself and is as free as before'. Indeed, he is more free, since he now has moral freedom, instead of natural freedom. Is the self thus realised or created? If it is realised, there should be a universal story to tell about reason and nature, with nature as the final arbiter; but politics could be essential to it. If it is created, then moral freedom is the freedom to live as one's community has shaped one truly to want to live, with the community as arbiter of what one truly wants. Both versions leave the self unclear, when we ask whether the 'I' is finally absorbed in the communal 'we' or distinct. Paradoxically, no doubt, it is both. The social conditions needed for the emergence of the General Will are those which release our true selves, each separately but all together. We then operate in unison, as we must if what emerges is truly to be the General Will and not a dangerous fiction. The General Will is not a collective discovery but a collective creation. On any particular matter, it is whatever emerges from the deliberations of a free people.

This resolution, however the politics of it are finally reckoned, looks ominous for dissenters, who, in being forced to obey the rulings of the General Will, are 'forced to be free'. So it is unsurprising that liberal thinkers in the Enlightenment line have never been sure whether Rousseau is friend or foe. But, for the purpose of deciding what reason is to say about trust, he challenges individualism at just the right depth. To make citizenship robust enough to underwrite trust, a society must be more than a club for self-interestedly rational individuals who want their backs scratched. Our sociality is less instrumental and more genuine than that.

So what more is needed? We have been led to propose a relative impartiality as the corrective to the partiality for which Hume sought a remedy in the judgement and understanding. That is what generalised reciprocity involves. Members have claims on members who owe nothing to them in particular. To make this stick, it is tempting to embed the self fully in its surrounding community. But reason jibs at once. Such deep embeddedness is too high a price for making fellow members trustworthy, as the double-edged example of honour makes plain. Local virtues which include being capable of promising often go with what Enlightenment condemns as vices; and locally approved individuality often reduces to an affirmation of loyalty to whatever community it is which tells people who they are and where they belong. So can we accept that norms are a source of reasons for reasonable persons without granting that reasonableness is finally relative to the local norms which give actions their meaning and people their bearings? Is there a form of association strong enough to secure trust but without requiring a local monopoly on what count as good reasons for acting in a trustworthy manner?

Here is what I take to be the best Enlightenment line of reply. Reciprocal relations like love, friendship, honour and patriotism extend the self into a wider community, which does indeed offer to settle who we are and where we belong. But they do not define us immutably, nor are schemes of generalised reciprocity beyond criticism. Entering a viable scheme of normative expectations goes with 'a remarkable change in man' but not all such schemes set us free. A community whose members recognise one another, and hence themselves, in service to others and yet retain their individuality is one thing; a community whose demands of loyalty are crushing is quite another. Pure communitarian thinking has to settle for purely local values. It deflects criticism from without by treating external critics as outsiders whose opinions lack *locus standi*. It thus licenses binding arrangements which conflict with, for instance, the UN declaration of basic human rights. That is intolerable to all reasonable men and women.

THE MORAL AND POLITICAL SCIENCES

Yet the Enlightenment Trail can be traversed only by those moved to act in partnership by a common good. That requires partial acceptance of a collective point of view. In miniature, this is teamwork, a temporary partnership seemingly too brief to threaten our individuality. But partnerships which are merely tactical do not overcome the problem of trust and the grand question remains whether the idea of a liberal community is a contradiction in terms. Can its members retain their critical distance while accepting their local obligations?

Part of the answer lies seemingly off the main trail, I think, since it depends on how we relate practical reason as conceived for purposes of social science to human freedom as conceived in ethics. Condorcet set out to console the philosopher who laments the errors, crimes and injustices which still pollute the earth. He looked forward to a time when the sun would shine only on free people whose only master was their reason and when the human race, freed from its shackles, would advance with a sure step along the path of truth, virtue and happiness. That is an exhilarating prospect, until we reflect on how it was to be achieved. Condorcet envisaged new moral and political sciences, equipped to reconcile the interests of each with the interests of all. Conflict, he assumed, was due to conflicting desires or imperfect institutions or both. His strategy was to identify suitable desires and to instil and regulate them with the aid of suitable institutions. With freedom defined negatively as the absence of impediments to desire, a society thus rationally organised would be a society of free people.

This programme includes planting a suitable idea of the good society in people's minds, as an aid to reconciling what they then come to regard as their interests. That makes it a highly manipulative exercise in social engineering and I am cheered if it founders on the problem of trust. Condorcet did not see the problem, because he thought that, since nature has endowed us with amiable sentiments along with 'ties of interest and duty', reason was simply revealing the path. But the picture changes abruptly, if we enter three large reservations about it. The first is that, since we have no reason to assume our natural sentiments to be predominantly amiable, it may be rash to clear away all obstacles to their flourishing. Secondly, if our interests are not all natural, we need to ask where the rest come from. Thirdly, we must consider the implications if 'ties of interest and duty' are a social engineer's way with failure to exclude unsociable preferences, while freedom is latently given a positive definition by the same engineer.

Critics of the Enlightenment project are thus entitled to worry that its liberalism is finally spurious or even that monsters are finally begotten not by the sleep of reason but by reason itself. A liberal community would indeed be a contradiction in terms, if the communal bond were engineered at the expense of individual freedom to form our own ideas. Yet, without a communal bond, the problem of trust resurfaces. Liberals thus face a dilemma. Shall they continue to espouse the fighting liberalism of the high Enlightenment, with its chain connecting truth, virtue and happiness, or shall they opt for a procedural liberalism, which separates the right from the good and breaks the links in the chain?

Current fashion tends to favour the latter. If it succeeds, the dilemma is easy to resolve by settling for constitutional ground rules which no reasonable person can reject. But it is proving notoriously difficult to maintain the fire-break between procedural and substantive values, between the right and the good. The procedural values turn out to be those of a substantive individualism, needing a metaphysical account of the self (even on the view taken in *Political Liberalism*, whose politics are different from its advice to liberals). Without a foray into matters of substance, one cannot explain to illiberal persons why liberalism is not one optional point of view among others. As democratic societies become more plural, intolerant persons and groups grow increasingly vocal and less inclined to accept an alleged overlapping historical consensus as binding. This means either the collapse of liberal societies or an enforcement of liberal values on grounds which reason cannot explain. Perhaps enforcement becomes more painless, as the moral and political sciences learn more about manipulation. But, either way, the upshot is not a liberal community.

Is there an alternative? Here is a suggestion. A fighting liberalism need not be an imposition, if the Enlightenment project can rethink the basis of the moral and political sciences. The starting point might be to regard the social world as an intersubjective fabric spun from shared meanings which persist or change as we negotiate their interpretation among ourselves. Relatedly, it is plausible to regard events as occurring in accordance with expectations, in the intriguing sense that, like price rises, victories and revolutions, they can happen because they are expected to happen. It is also plausible to suggest that both the predictive and the normative kinds of expectation can have this effect, thus injecting interpretive and creative elements into the story of social life. The more we think in these terms, the more the social sciences need a method of *Verstehen*, which sees the construct through the eyes of social actors because its reality depends on how they come to see it.

Such an approach will find itself linking truth, virtue and happiness, but not as Condorcet did. They are linked in the first instance because there are connections in the people's minds between what is and what ought to be. But this is merely to say that, in understanding a social world, one must know how its inhabitants understand it. In the second instance, however, we note that their understanding is in part theoretical and thus realise the power of the social sciences to influence this understanding by putting ideas into people's minds. Hence the social sciences are, so to speak, tied to their own tails. Whether their hypotheses are true depends partly but irreducibly on whether they carry conviction with the social actors whose activity they analyse.

That makes political science, no less than politics itself, the art of the possible. The same can be said, less epigrammatically, of the other social sciences. At first sight, there can be a value-neutral social science, because values can be studied neutrally. On reflection, values are imbued with theorising, and ideas about how social life can and should be organised are part of its intersubjective reality.

This alternative approach has limits, however, and it is vital to stress them for two reasons. One is that, since wishing something were is not usually enough to bring it about, ideas are not enough to make real magic. We cannot become healthy, wealthy or wise just by believing that we are. Images may make a virtual reality but not one which feeds the poor or gives power to the weak. A social science so drunk on constructions that it simply equates construction with reality is as dangerous as it is incomplete. The other reason is that relativism has bad versions as well as good and they need distinguishing. The good ones recognise the internal, perspectival character of social objects humanly viewed. The bad ones go on to infer that any integrated, shared view is both true and justified. The difference has to lie in the thought that perspective is not the end of the story.

This is plain for the natural world and natural sciences, even if one presumes that observing affects what is observed. When a meteor strikes Earth, interpreters are no safer than their cameras. But the double hermeneutic in the social sciences can seem to make a difference. It seems to internalise not only the social dimension of social facts but even the criteria for organising and judging the internalisation. Yet it must not do so if disputes about truth are to remain possible. This would hold even if they were thought to be predicated merely on consistency, since consistency makes no sense without reference to truth and needs supplementing before it can govern concepts in, say, sociology. Hence constructions need something which is not constructed. Since that seems impossible to empiricists and post-empiricists, an *impasse* seems to have been reached.

But it is not impossible, if one grants that a strongly rationalist account of the *a priori* is still in the field. This is one which takes it that we have *a priori* knowledge or, more subtly, that our needing it is sufficient for our knowing that we have it. Either way, the case is that otherwise all our thinking becomes incoherent, since it becomes stuck in a self-refuting relativism. We would then be landed with wondering whether what we take for *a priori* is truly so in a language which pre-supposes it. Although we can ask if some regarded propositions are beyond doubt as claimed, we can do so only if not all can be doubted. Those immune, because true, include those which make doubt poss-ible. This may seem to empiricists to involve a circle which forfeits the game. But that is because empiricism has no alternative, even though its own incoherence shows that it needs one. Pragmatism, on the other hand, grants the point and hopes to blunt it by refusing to accept any ultimate analytic–synthetic distinction or coherent deeper reason for one. But the point granted is larger than the reservation can cancel, unless it is taken seriously enough to lead either back to empiricism or on to rationalism.[5]

This has to be a tentative view, in need of further reflection. But I see no other way to make sense of Kant's reasons for the uniqueness of the categories or, at least, to make further speculation possible. In upshot, the creative element in expectations works a limited magic and theorising influences expectations. The magic is limited partly because interpretation still has to relate to a world which settles whether people starve and die, even if that is an interpreted world, and partly because creativity is limited by reason. But theories of social life can recognise that people are theorists of social life, provided that social life is thus made perspectival, rather than fully self-warranting. To this extent and in this precise sense, the social sciences are indeed grist to their own mill.

5. For my view of the related dangers of going overboard for a 'strong programme' in the sociology of knowledge, see 'The social destruction of reality' in M. Hollis and S. Lukes (eds.), *Rationality and Relativism*, Oxford: Basil Blackwell, 1982.

That prompts a final comment on the thought which we met at the start of the Enlightenment Trail, when asking whether reason strengthens the bond of society or undermines it. I endorse the fear that instrumental, 'economic' rationality can destroy trust, and hence, among other ties, the trust which markets need too. Putting this account of rationality into people's minds as a scientifically true account tends to have the sad effect of helping it come truer. But it does not make it true, because it breaches the limits to what can be consistently believed. Conversely, therefore, reasoning them out of it makes it less influential; and reasoning them into a rival account of trust in a well ordered society makes a well ordered society likelier to come about. Since this latter proposition involves no incoherence, we can finally transcend our human limitations as we flesh it out.

In seeing ourselves as persons with interdependent reasons for action, we clear the way for a liberal society as a community where trust is secured by mutual respect and generalised reciprocity among reasonable persons. Such a normative approach makes it possible to distinguish the genuinely civic virtues from those which are merely functional for a viable but hegemonic society. To be clear about the true character of reason in human affairs and in the human sciences is thus the beginning of wisdom on a path which, properly constructed, is one of truth, virtue and happiness and leads to The Triumph of Reason. This is definitely a matter where philosophy does not yield to Condorcet's idea of science. Even if 'all errors in politics and morals are based on philosophical errors', it is not true that all philosophical errors 'result from scientific errors'. How consoling for the philosopher!

CITIZENS OF THE WORLD?

So the idea of a liberal community is not a contradiction in terms. Yet trust is growing fragile in today's world. Is that because we are becoming more rational or less? The Enlightenment answer is still that reason can cure social ills and spread trust as we grow more rational. So, even if there are other ways to trust, this one lies along the Enlightenment Trail, thus avoiding the snags of the rest. But all depends on defining reason aright. We must both agree with Condorcet that reason shows how 'truth, virtue and happiness are bound together by an unbreakable chain' and deny that reason is reporting a prior fact.

Trust comes in two kinds, predictive and normative (or expecting that and expecting of) and the latter holds the key. That first emerged when we asked how strategically minded actors can advance along the Enlightenment Trail. The puzzle was how to stop backward induction making the walk end at The Rational Choice. The answer seemed to be that there is no problem, provided that the trail has no known limit, for instance because the game will be repeated or played with others who know what happened on the initial occasion. But the crux was still how rational choice theory standardly abstracts and idealises. At its heart there lies an egoism, even if it is rightly taken as a philosophical, not a psychological, egoism. Yet, if only the agent's passions motivate and are met only by the consequences of satisfying them, then the trail is closed.

To spell this out, we turned to Hobbes and Hume – a self guided by fear or sympathy or both. Fear is Hobbes' solution, generalised to include other sanctions like social disapproval. But we can often escape sanctions in a society like ours, where most of us no longer believe in metaphysical penalties, like those of religion, and all of us sometimes have Gyges' ring of invisibility. The foole has an unanswerable point in suggesting that he and other Hobbesian people cannot be trusted. Hume then mutes the point by adding motives of sympathy for others. But, as he says himself when introducing the sensible knave, this makes us care only about those we know and like. While reason remains the slave of the passions, even neighbouring farmers may have no reason to trust each other, even though both then lose their harvests for want of mutual confidence and security.

More generally, egoism gives no basis for impersonal trust. Even if one had an egoistic reason to play fair with a stranger, it would be only when one had no better reason not to. That would make trust a merely practical question. But there is a different question about whether this is the right account of reason. Are those who are trustworthy when they have no egoistic reason irrational? Is the key the extent of information and the prospect of further encounters where one's previous conduct is known or is it a different idea of reason or is it that the secret of trust lies beyond reason?

The first answer would make rational people more trustworthy on a more limited range of occasions; but it would leave many occasions to rat and would undermine people with irrational motives. Promising, in particular, is not accounted for by stability, since it depends on more than ultimately forward-looking reasons.

So the second answer is better – that trust makes sense, given a different idea of reason. Hence many people, deemed irrational by the first answer, are in truth rational. But what is the new account? A Kantian answer is attractive, especially because it shows how reasons can bind impartially *in foro interno*. Yet few trust for this austerely moral reason and, in any case, we would not want the removal of the conditional element in trust which adopting Kant brings about. Conditional reasons are not Kantian moral ones. But they are, so to speak, quasi-moral and, if we deny the previous egoism, can be impersonally good reasons. This suggests a new basis for rational action, owing something to Kant and something to the idea of generalised reciprocity. Neither element is consistent with contractarianism or with contractarian ways of trying to combine them, since self-interest cannot be transmuted into even a quasi-morality and generalised reciprocity is not a version of self-interest.

But this does not make Kant and generalised reciprocity combinable. So we tried replacing Kantian individuals by more located and conditional agents. Could individualism allow enough to Wittgensteinian thinking or liberalism to communitarianism? Well, there are indeed 'games' of social life, with rules constitutive as well as regulative, and constitutive rules might be dubbed 'quasi-moral'. But this does more to set a problem than to solve one. They are intersubjective, internally binding and yet not necessarily moral. Thus a *mafioso* or cannibal has a reason internally and intersubjectively, but not externally to social relations which we reserve the right and ability to question. We are embedded in games of social life but not lost in them, as the examples of honour and cannibalism show. Individualism may perhaps come to terms with a Wittgensteinian belief that essentially social actors are still separately active but a liberal cannot agree to as much as a communitarian demands. The rational basis of trust remains a problem.

So how can we best work out what Hume termed 'a remedy, in the judgement and understanding, for what is irregular and incommodious in the affections'? To get rational agents thinking in terms of joint enterprises, we can propose teamwork. To keep them rational, we can have them acting not as a new mystical unit but as agents who put the collective enterprise first. This goes with our being 'reasonable persons' and equipped with more than forward-looking reasons. But we shall need a tricky idea of persons, as foreshadowed by Rousseau's 'remarkable change in man', so as to make generalised reciprocity possible. Generalised reciprocity is what makes sense of vendettas, of lifts offered to hitch-hikers and of blood donation: C helps D because A has helped B. So it is still unclear whether this is possible for liberals who agree with Condorcet that 'truth, virtue and happiness are bound together by an indissoluble chain'. In dropping the line between right and good, not least because the right is not merely procedural, they cannot give every community the right to dictate to its members. Present ignorance is not enough of a block and, in any case, the wrong sort of block. No doubt it helps to regard the good as in part a construct, rather than a discovery. But, if it were solely a construct, all sorts of further trouble would arise. Nor, if all reduces to a struggle for who determines the kind of construct, can liberalism always win.

In sum, therefore, we need to say that liberals are citizens of the world which they construct on liberal principles. They subscribe to a communitarian idea about persons but trump it by insisting that communities must accept liberal ideas about universal demands of the right and the good. These demands are left deliberately incomplete. That the good and the right are inseparable and universal does not mean that they go into universal detail. Nor could they, if a constructivism is right for the area of detail. So a well-ordered society can indeed be founded on a truth of reason, which stands outside any construct and serves as a criterion, and there is a universal positive story to tell about freedom. But the universal element is incomplete along with the detail of the freedom, thus leaving a realm where construction rules. Practical wisdom thus relies on a constructivist understanding of free action and the common good, while also submitting its constructions to a universal and *a priori* test of truth. That gives a universal basis for trust between reasonable persons. It makes citizens what liberals have always hoped – finally citizens of the world.

Conclusion

A fighting arrogance about questions must still go with a proper humility about answers. The triumph of reason lies in an uncertain future, partly because liberals have yet to agree on the character of positive freedom and partly because its detail is too much a construct to enforce. But we have enough to go on. Adam and Eve can still head along the Enlightenment Trail in trust-within-reason. The trail still ends at The Triumph of Reason.

BIBLIOGRAPHY

Altham, J. E. J. and Harrison, R. (eds.) *World, Mind and Ethics*, Cambridge University Press, 1995.

Arrow, K. J. *Social Choice and Individual Values*, 2nd edition, New Haven: Yale University Press, 1963.

Axelrod, R. *The Evolution of Cooperation*, New York: Basic Books, 1984.

Baier, Annette 'Trust and anti-trust', *Ethics*, 96 (1986), pp. 231–60.

Baker, Judith 'Trust and rationality', *Pacific Philosophical Quarterly*, 68 (1987), pp. 1–13.

Becker, Gary *The Economic Approach to Human Behavior*, University of Chicago Press, 1976.

Bentham, Jeremy *An Introduction to the Principles of Morals and Legislation* (1789), London: Athlone Press, 1970.

Binmore, K. G. 'Bargaining and morality', in Gauthier and Sugden (eds.), *Rationality, Justice and the Social Contract* (1993).

Blau, Peter *Exchange and Power in Social Life*, New York: John Wiley, 1964.

Blum, L. A. *Friendship, Altruism and Morality*, London: Routledge and Kegan Paul, 1980.

Bonanno, G. 'The logic of rational play in games of perfect information', *Economics & Philosophy*, 7 (1991), pp. 37–65.

Bond, E. J. *Reason and Value*, Cambridge University Press, 1983.

Buchanan, J. M. and Tullock, G. *The Calculus of Consent*, Ann Arbor: University of Michigan Press, 1962.

Campbell, R and Sowden, L. (eds.) *Paradoxes of Rationality and Cooperation*, Vancouver: University of British Columbia Press, 1985.

Condorcet, Marquis de *Sketch For a Historical Picture of the Human Mind* (1795), ed. Stuart Hampshire, trans. June Barraclough, Westport, Conn.: Greenwood Press, 1955.

Dasgupta, P. 'Trust as a commodity', in Gambetta (ed.), *Trust* (1988).

Edgeworth, F. Y. *Mathematical Psychics*, London: Kegan Paul, 1881.

Elster, J. *Ulysses and the Sirens*, Cambridge University Press, 1979.

Elster, J. and Hylland, A. (eds.) *Foundations of Social Choice Theory*, Cambridge University Press, 1986.

Farina, S., Hahn, F. and Vannucci, S. (eds.) *Ethics, Rationality and Economic Behaviour*, Oxford: Clarendon Press, 1996.

Frankfurt, H. G. 'Freedom of the will and the concept of a person', *Journal of Philosophy*, 68 (1971), reprinted in Frankfurt, *The Importance of What We Care About* (1988).

The Importance of What We Care About, Cambridge University Press, 1988.

'On the usefulness of final ends', *Iyyun: The Jerusalem Philosophical Quarterly*, 41 (1992), pp. 3–19.

'On the necessity of ideals', in Noam and Wesen (eds.), *The Moral Self* (1993).

'Autonomy, necessity and love', in Fulda and Horstmann (eds.), *Vernunftbegriffe in der Moderne* (1994).

Fukuyama, Francis *Trust: The Social Virtues and the Creation of Prosperity*, New York: The Free Press, 1995.

Fulda, H. and Horstmann, R.-P. (eds.) *Vernunftbegriffe in der Moderne*, Stuttgart: Klett-Cotta, 1994.

Gambetta, Diego 'Mafia: the price of distrust', in Gambetta (ed.), *Trust* (1988).

Gambetta, Diego (ed.) *Trust: Making and Breaking Cooperative Relations*, Oxford: Basil Blackwell, 1988.

Gauthier, David 'Coordination', *Dialogue*, 14 (1975), pp. 195–221.

Morals by Agreement, Oxford University Press, 1986.

'Commitment and choice: an essay on the rationality of plans', in Farina, Hahn and Vannucci (eds.), *Ethics, Rationality and Economic Behaviour* (1996).

Gauthier, David and Sugden, Robert (eds.) *Rationality, Justice and the Social Contract*, Hemel Hempstead: Harvester Wheatsheaf, 1993.

Gilbert, Margaret *On Social Facts*, London: Routledge, 1989.

Govier, Trudy 'An epistemology of trust', *International Journal of Moral and Social Studies*, 8 (1993), pp. 155–74.

Hampshire, Stuart (ed.) *Public and Private Morality*, Cambridge University Press, 1978.

Hardin, R. *Collective Action*, Baltimore: Johns Hopkins University Press, 1982.

Hargreave Heap, S. Hollis, M., Lyons, B., Sugden, R. and Weale, A. (eds.) *The Theory of Choice: A Critical Guide*, Oxford: Blackwell, 1992.

Harrison, R. (ed.) *Rational Action*, Cambridge University Press, 1979.

Harsanyi, J. C. *Rational Behaviour and Bargaining Equilibrium in Games and Social Situations*, Cambridge University Press, 1977.

Harsanyi, J. C. and Selten, R. *A General Theory of Equilibrium Selection in Games*, Cambridge, Mass.: MIT Press, 1988.

Heath, A. *Rational Choice and Social Exchange*, Cambridge University Press, 1976.

Held, Virginia 'On the meaning of "trust"', *Ethics*, 78 (1968), pp. 156–9.

Hobbes, Thomas *Leviathan* (1651), ed. R. Tuck, Cambridge University Press, 1991.

Hollis, Martin *Models of Man: Philosophical Thoughts on Social Action*, Cambridge University Press 1977.

'Rational man and social science', in Harrison (ed.), *Rational Action* (1979).

'The social destruction of reality', in Hollis and Lukes (eds.), *Rationality and Relativism* (1982).

The Cunning of Reason, Cambridge University Press, 1988.

'Moves and motives', *Analysis*, 50 (1990), pp. 49–62, reprinted in Hollis, *Reason in Action* (1996).

'Penny pinching and backward induction', *Journal of Philosophy*, 88 (1991), pp. 473–88.

'The agriculture of the mind', in Gauthier and Sugden (eds.), *Rationality, Justice and the Social Contract* (1993).

'The shape of a life', in Altham and Harrison (eds.), *World, Mind and Ethics* (1995).

'Honour among thieves', in Hollis, *Reason in Action* (1996).

Reason in Action, Cambridge University Press, 1996.

Hollis, Martin and Nell, E. *Rational Economic Man*, Cambridge University Press, 1975.

Hollis, Martin and Sugden, Robert 'Rationality in action', *Mind*, 102 (1993), pp. 1–35.

Hollis, Martin and Lukes, S. (eds.) *Rationality and Relativism*, Oxford: Basil Blackwell, 1982.

Hume, David *A Treatise of Human Nature* (1739), ed. P. H. Nidditch, Oxford: Clarendon Press, 1978.

An Enquiry Concerning Human Understanding (1748), ed. P. H. Nidditch, Oxford: Clarendon Press, 1975.

An Enquiry Concerning the Principles of Morals (1751), ed. P. H. Nidditch, Oxford: Clarendon Press, 1975.

Hurley, S. *Natural Reasons*, Oxford University Press, 1989.

Jevons, W. S. *The Theory of Political Economy* (1871), Harmondsworth: Penguin Books, 1970.

Kant, Immanuel 'Idea for a universal history with a cosmopolitan purpose' (1784), in *Kant's Political Writings*, ed. Hans Reiss, trans. H. B. Nisbet, Cambridge University Press, 1970.

Lewin, Leif and Vedung, Evert (eds.) *Politics and Rational Action*, Dordrecht: Reidel, 1980.

Lewis, David *Convention: A Philosophical Study*, Cambridge, Mass.: Harvard University Press, 1969.

Locke, John *Essays on the Law of Nature* (1663), ed. W. von Leyden, Oxford: Clarendon Press, 1954.

An Essay Concerning Human Understanding (1690), ed. P. H. Nidditch, Oxford: Clarendon Press, 1975.

Luce, R. D. and Raiffa, H. *Games and Decisions*, New York: John Wiley, 1957.

Margolis, J. *Selfishness, Altruism and Rationality*, Cambridge University Press, 1982.

Mason, John Hope 'Individuals in society: Rousseau's republican vision', in *History of Political Thought*, 10 (1989), pp. 89–112.

McDowell, John 'Might there be external reasons?', in Altham and Harrison (eds.), *World, Mind and Ethics* (1995).

McLennen, Edward *Rationality and Dynamic Choice*, Cambridge University Press, 1990.

Mill, John Stuart *Utilitarianism* (1861), Everyman edition, London: J. M. Dent & Sons, 1972.

Nagel, Thomas *The Possibility of Altruism*, Oxford University Press, 1970.

'Rawls on justice', *Philosophical Review*, 82 (1973), pp. 226–34.

'Ruthlessness in public life', in Hampshire (ed.), *Public and Private Morality* (1978).

The View From Nowhere, Oxford University Press, 1986.

Nash. J. F. 'The bargaining problem', *Econometrica*, 18 (1950), pp. 155–62.

'Two person cooperative games', *Econometrica*, 21 (1953), pp. 128–40.

Neumann, J. von and Morgenstern, O. *Theory of Games and Economic Behavior*, 2nd edition, Princeton University Press, 1947.

Nietzsche, Friedrich *The Genealogy of Morals* (1887), New York: Doubleday, 1956.

Noam, G. C. and Wesen, T. *The Moral Self*, Cambridge, Mass.: MIT Press, 1993.

Nussbaum, Martha *The Fragility of Goodness*, Cambridge University Press, 1986.

O'Hagan, T. *The End of Law?* Oxford: Basil Blackwell, 1984.

Olson, M. *The Logic of Collective Action*, Cambridge, Mass.: Harvard University Press, 1965.

Pareto, Vilfredo *Manual of Political Economy* (1927), trans. A. S. Schweir, London: Macmillan, 1972.

Parfit, Derek *Reasons and Persons*, Oxford: Clarendon Press, 1984.

Pearce, D. 'Rationalizable strategic behavior and the problem of perfection', *Econometrica*, 52 (1984), pp. 1029–50.

Pettit, Philip 'The cunning of trust', *Philosophy and Public Affairs*, 24 (1995), pp. 202–25.

Pettit, Philip and Sugden, Robert 'The backward induction paradox', *Journal of Philosophy*, 86 (1989), pp. 169–82.

Ramsey, Frank *The Foundations of Mathematics and Other Logical Essays*, London: Routledge and Kegan Paul, 1931.

Rapoport, A. *Two-Person Game Theory*, Ann Arbor: University of Michigan Press, 1966.

Rasmusen, E. *Games and Information*, Oxford: Basil Blackwell, 1989.

Rawls, John *A Theory of Justice*, Cambridge, Mass.: Harvard University Press, 1971.

'Justice as fairness: political and metaphysical', *Philosophy and Public Affairs*, 14 (1985), pp. 223–51, reprinted in Rawls, *Political Liberalism 1993*).

Political Liberalism, New York: Columbia University Press, 1993.

Riker, William H. 'Political trust as rational choice', in Lewin and Verdung (eds.), *Political and Rational Action* (1980).

Rousseau, Jean-Jacques *The Social Contract* (1762), in *Collected Writings of Rousseau, Volume 4*, ed. Roger D. Masters and Christopher Kelly, Dartmouth, N.H.: University Press of New England, 1994.

Samuelson, Paul *Foundations of Economic Analysis*, Cambridge, Mass.: Harvard University Press, 1947.

Savage, Leonard *The Foundations of Statistics*, New York: John Wiley, 1954.

Schelling, T. C. *The Strategy of Conflict*, Cambridge, Mass.: Harvard University Press, 1960.

Choice and Consequence, Cambridge, Mass.: Harvard University Press, 1984.

Schick, F. *Having Reasons: An Essay on Rationality and Sociality*, Princeton University Press, 1984.

Searle, John *The Construction of Social Reality*, Harmondsworth: Allen Lane, The Penguin Press, 1995.

Selten, R. (ed.) *Rational Interaction: Essays in Honor of John C. Harsanyi*, Berlin: Springer-Verlag, 1992.

Sen, A. K. *Collective Choice and Social Welfare*, London: Oliver & Boyd, 1970.

'Rational fools', *Philosophy and Public Affairs*, 6 (1977), pp. 317–44, reprinted in Sen, *Choice, Welfare and Measurement* (1982).

Choice, Welfare and Measurement, Oxford: Basil Blackwell, 1982.

Sheffrin, S. M. *Rational Expectations*, Cambridge University Press, 1983.

Smith, Adam *The Theory of Moral Sentiments* (1759), ed. D. Raphael and A. Macfie, Oxford: Clarendon Press, 1976.

Sugden, Robert 'Rational choice: a survey of contributions from economics and philosophy', *Economic Journal*, 101 (1991), pp. 751–85.

'Inductive reasoning in repeated games', in Selten (ed.), *Rational Interaction* (1992).

'Rational coordination', in Farina, Hahn and Vannucci (eds.), *Ethics, Rationality and Economic Behaviour* (1996).

Sutton, J. 'Non-cooperative bargaining theory: an introduction', *Review of Economic Studies*, 53 (1986), pp. 709–24.

Taylor, M. *Anarchy and Cooperation*, Chichester: John Wiley, 1976.

The Possibility of Cooperation, Cambridge University Press, 1987.

Thomas, D. O. 'The duty of trust', *Proceedings of the Aristotelian Society*, 79 (1978), pp. 89–101.

Titmuss, R. M. *The Gift Relationship: From Human Blood to Social Policy*, London: Allen and Unwin, 1970.

Tuomela, Raimo *The Importance of Us*, Stanford University Press, 1995.

Watson, Gary 'Free agency', *Journal of Philosophy*, 72 (1975), pp. 205–20.

Weber, Max *Economy and Society*, ed. G. Roth and C. Wittich, New York: Bedminster Press, 1968.

Williams, Bernard *Moral Luck*, Cambridge University Press, 1981.

Ethics and the Limits of Philosophy, London: Fontana Books, 1985.

'Values, reasons and the theory of persuasion', in Farina, Hahn and Vannucci (eds.), *Ethics, Rationality and Economic Behaviour* (1996).

Wittgenstein, Ludwig *Philosophical Investigations*, Oxford: Basil Blackwell, 1953.

INDEX